MW00416771

"A roadmap for those topics we're trained to avoid. Skot takes the most complicated matters of life and offers simple and profound clarity through Scripture and personal testimony. The takeaways in this book are numerous and compose the recipe for the Christocentric life those who believe are thirsting for."

Katie Appold, MPA, owner, Nonprofit Nav; executive director, AIRS; adjunct professor of nonprofit leadership, Cornerstone University

"Jesus prayed in John 17:21 that the church would be one. As Christians who are in pursuit of God's will, we have to eventually deal with the things that are keeping us from being united as the body of Christ. In *Unfractured*, Skot Welch opens the dialogue about how the identity crisis we have as Christians keeps us divided, and he helps us center ourselves on Christ, without whom no unity is possible."

Joel Brooks Jr., pastor, Stones Church, Kalamazoo and Grand Rapids, Michigan

"In this urgently needed book, Skot Welch delivers both a prophetic punch and a practical action plan for cultural change in a world of increasing division. As you read, you'll be troubled, encouraged, changed."

Jeff Crosby, publishing executive; author, *The Language of the Soul*

"Despite the increasing desire of organizations to build diverse teams, the value of diversity and the ways forward often need to be clarified. *Unfractured* presents Skot's knowledge of diversity and cultural intelligence from his lived experiences and life as a black professional. His approach is intriguing, thought-provoking, and practical."

Terumi Echols, president and publisher, InterVarsity Press

"Skot Welch is a steady and reconciling voice. His newest book, *Unfractured*, is filled with research, reasoning, and warmth. It pierces without polarizing. It's theological and thoughtful and shows us the better way as Christians living in a divided world."

Scott Hagan, PhD, president, North Central University

"Some may take offense at this book's honest and often uncomfortable approach to religious racism. But if you're ready for a hard conversation that will renew your mind and align your heart with the heart of God, you won't do better than to read this beautiful book by my friend Skot Welch."

Stan Jantz, CEO, Come and See Foundation

"*Unfractured* dares to push Christians into a new era by challenging us to embrace our true Christ-centered identity. Once we start walking in the identity that Christ intended for us, we can truly shift the culture. *Unfractured* lays out practical and actionable steps for us to get there."

Xavier "X" Jernigan, The Voice of Spotify; deacon,
Emmanuel Baptist Church, Brooklyn, New York

"*Unfractured* is the racial-unity book the church needs. Welch provides a Gospel-centered framework that helps leaders work against racism, toward unity. With uncompromising biblical understanding of human value and a call to action against deceptions that would cause Christians to devalue life, Welch provides tangible actions to unfracture the kingdom."

Dr. Desirée Libengood, associate vice president of academics,
North Central University

"I count it an honor to call Skot a personal mentor. Over the years, I have witnessed how these thoughts like having a Christocentric, ethnoconscious identity have transformed church culture. Skot's grace, patience, and love allow a rare opportunity for this trusted guide to help churches navigate this sensitive space."

Rich Nibbe, executive pastor, NPHX Church, Phoenix, Arizona

"Skot has reminded us that we were put on earth to serve God with everyone, everywhere, and in everything, unto God. Thank you, Skot, for bringing us back to our true identity, and for challenging us to remember that we all have a purpose and plan on earth. We are uniquely and wonderfully made, and we thank you for this book that is a work of heart for us all."

Janis Petrini, Purpose Driven Talent

"Skot Welch has written a timely and powerful book that challenges us to rethink how we talk about race and ethnicity in the church and beyond. With biblical insight and practical wisdom, he shows us how to celebrate our diversity, embrace a new kingdom language, and engage in compassionate conversations that lead to reconciliation. This book is a must-read for anyone who wants to be part of God's redemptive solution for our broken world."

Samuel Rodriguez, lead pastor, New Season; president and CEO, National Hispanic Christian Leadership Conference; author, *Your Mess, God's Miracle*; executive producer, *Breakthrough* and *Flamin' Hot*

"For those interested in experiencing the transformational power of a unified church, you must read *Unfractured*. Skot Welch draws on years of diversity, equity, and inclusion experience to provide powerful insights and effective tools for us to heal fractures caused by secular influences and cultural differences to become a unified church."

Deloris S. Thomas, PhD, president, Joseph Business School

# Unfractured

# Unfractured

## A Christ-Centered **Action Plan** for **Cultural Change**

**Skot Welch**

*a division of Baker Publishing Group*
Minneapolis, Minnesota

Published by Chosen Books
Minneapolis, Minnesota
www.chosenbooks.com

Chosen Books is a division of
Baker Publishing Group, Grand Rapids, Michigan

Printed in the United States of America



ISBN 978-0-8007-6354-1 (cloth)
ISBN 978-1-4934-4252-2 (ebook)

Library of Congress Cataloging-in-Publication Control Number: 2023010857



Cover design by Studio Gearbox

The author is represented by the literary agency of AuthorizeMe Literary Firm LLC.

Baker Publishing Group publications use paper produced from sustainable forestry practices and post-consumer waste whenever possible.

23 24 25 26 27 28 29 7 6 5 4 3 2 1

To my "Ever Mores"—
The love of my life, my wife, Barbara,
and my wonderful children Brandon and Brooks.
You exhibit, daily and for "ever more,"
God's heart for me. I love you.

To my precious family—
Aunts and uncles (surrogate parents)
and to my mom, who is now in heaven,
who have loved me unconditionally from Day 1.
Also, my mom- and dad-in-love
(as well as my other in-loves—brothers and sisters),
my dad, my awesome sister, and a host of cousins,
nieces, and nephews. You are my heart.

To my mentors/pastors—
Thank you for always being there for me,
helping me to mature, and speaking into my life—
and for speaking life into me.

## Additional Resources (and Sounds)

For resources including an "Unfractured Sonic Landscape" playlist on Spotify, deeper-dive podcasts, as well as information on how to become a certified facilitator of the *Unfractured* curriculum, scan this QR code:

# Contents

# Acknowledgments

To Him who was, who is, and who is to come.

The power of this book is the result of God's grace and help.

The beauty of this book is that God's grace and help was clearly shown through the love, expertise, and insight of the wonderful people He brought across my path to bring it to fruition.

*And the list below is just an excerpt:*

Thank you to Stan Jantz, Jeff Crosby, and my ECPA (Evangelical Christian Publishers Association) family for allowing me to be a part of the discussion as you lean in further to help your members model the Mosaic of God.

Thank you to Kim Bangs and my wonderful Baker Publishing/Chosen family for believing in this project and encouraging me to do all that God had put in my heart to do.

Thank you to Sharon Elliott of AuthorizeMe Literary Firm for being such a great (and patient) writing coach, editor, agent, and friend.

Thank you to Eric Johnson of Gorilla (Films) for being so consistent and steadfast in helping me to imagine the bigger version of this project.

Thank you to Jeffrey Wright of Urban Ministries, Inc. for always providing great perspective at the formation of the idea that became the book.

Thank you to John Common of Intelligent Demand for helping me to think more clearly about the reader beyond the pews.

Thank you to my family at Ada Bible Church for always being open to challenging Kingdom conversations about God's heart for all of God's people.

Thank you to Joyce Dinkins and my family at Our Daily Bread Ministries for being an important catalyst of this project.

Thank you to my family at North Central University for being exactly the type of champions God needs in the heart of Minneapolis.

Thank you to my Stones Church/Christian Life Center family who are, quite simply, some of the most wonderful and beautiful people I know who connect people to God, people to people and heaven to earth.

And finally, to all of you who want to live an "Unfractured" life for Christ, I thank God for you.

You make Him smile.

# Preface

## A New Language for a New Church Era . . . For God's Family

What do you think of when you hear the word *language*? I know what I think of: the funny story my friend Sharon shared with me about her introduction to the French language as a college freshman. As a native English speaker majoring in Spanish because she hoped to enter the world of elementary education in California in the late '70s, for some reason, the university required her to enroll in classes of yet another language.

Each day, Sharon moved from her 10 a.m. Conversational Spanish 300 class to her 11 a.m. Introduction to French 102. To make matters worse, the professor did not allow anyone to speak anything but French in class. Sharon thought *oui* would be pronounced "oo-we" instead of simply "we," and she was completely thrown off by the silent letters. For example, *Bordeaux* is pronounced bore-doh instead of "bore-dee-aux." And she had thought English was weird.

Nevertheless, she managed to get an *A* in that class because the teacher was just that good at using hand signals, a pointer, and repetition. Sharon eventually changed her major to liberal studies, and taught successfully for thirty-five years in California—as an English teacher. The moral of the story for her: Language and mastery take time, and we are all in different places in our journey. We should be patient with each other and with ourselves.

I tend to agree. Language is more than the different tongues spoken by varying cultures around the world. Language is a tool for effective communication. And with so many languages, one would think we'd be able to get our ideas across to each other. But unfortunately, in our current social environment, and especially amongst the body of Christ, when it comes to effectively communicating the unity we should be displaying to the world, we are running around like the folks at the Tower of Babel who had just had their language changed. As long as their language was the same, they were of one purpose—building a tower to reach to heaven to make a name for themselves. The problem was, in their case, they weren't supposed to be making a name for themselves. They were supposed to be living in a way to honor God's name, so God put a stop to their efforts by confusing their language. When they discovered they could no longer connect verbally, they found others who talked like they did—who spoke the same language—and headed off to establish their own communities, leaving the tower as an unfinished reminder of their folly.

The society of Babel was fractured because of the people's inability to communicate.

The church is fractured today because of people's inability to communicate. But thanks to the unifying blood of Jesus, this fact does not have to remain true. God has given us a tower to build—His kingdom. The completion of the building on earth is our responsibility and can only be done as we learn to communicate effectively as one body, the church. The family.

But we have problems. Strained racial and ethnic relations, deceptions of various sorts of "privilege," low esteem, and the like have driven a wedge between segments of the church—between the "black church" and the "white church" specifically—that has effectively separated us for so long that decidedly different languages have developed. And unfortunately, we seem to be just fine with this reality. However, I don't think God is. Romans 12:4–5 says, "Just as each of us has one body with many members, and these members do not all have the same function, so in Christ we, though many, form one body, and each member belongs to all the others" (NIV).

Diversity, you see, is God's idea. He obviously enjoys it, or He wouldn't have created it in the first place. But when our differences (e.g., ethnic, denominational, political) take precedence over God's Word, and we bow at the altar of those man-made distinctions instead of at the foot of the Cross, we have a big problem. This is where we are today. We cannot work together as a body until we are able to communicate effectively. Until the fracture is fixed.

So, here's a new language for a new church era. The explanations of truths, understandings, and change suggestions herein will reverse the trend of separation so the body of Christ can function as an unfractured whole, bringing glory to our God, who can then operate on our planet through the unity of His family. Let's enroll in class and learn a new language, shall we?

# See False Identities

When you received Christ, how did that recalibrate your thinking and change your life? Did it mean a change from a lifestyle you were following or from the culture you were in? Since becoming a Christ-follower, what culture have you continued to live in? Do you still follow that culture, perhaps even at the expense of your allegiance to Christ? Have you paid much attention to your new identity as a Christian, or is your life much the same as it was BC (before Christ)? Your true identity is who you are in Christ. We are called to be Christ-followers.

God had you in mind when He "created the heavens and the earth" (Genesis 1:1). He created this beautiful ecosystem—the earth, the stars, the sea, and vegetation—all for humans, for you and me (Genesis 1:1–2:2). God said everything created was good but reserved an extra exclamation for His creation of humans. Look at how Genesis 1:26–29 (CSB) relates this part of the story:

> Then God said, "Let us make man in our image, according to our likeness. They will rule the fish of the sea, the birds of the sky,

the livestock, the whole earth, and the creatures that crawl on the earth."

So, God created man
in his own image:
he created him in the image of God;
he created them male and female.

God blessed them, and God said to them, "Be fruitful, multiply, fill the earth, and subdue it. Rule the fish of the sea, the birds of the sky, and every creature that crawls on the earth." God also said, "Look, I have given you every seed-bearing plant on the surface of the entire earth and every tree whose fruit contains seed. This will be food for you, for all the wildlife of the earth, for every bird of the sky, and for every creature that crawls on the earth—everything having the breath of life in it—I have given every green plant for food." And it was so. God saw all that He had made, and it was very good indeed. When God got to that point in the creative work—when He created human beings—God said, "Wow, that's *very* good!"

Think about God's "wow." God was overjoyed when He made you and me. We are human beings completely adored by our Heavenly Father, even though we're imperfect because of the Fall. Adam's disobedience made him the progenitor of all human beings to follow, and he passed to us a sin nature that never should have been a part of our identity. Through Christ we find our true identity, and that new, true identity is the part of us that connects heaven to earth.

## Understanding Identity

Now, our sinful identity and Christ's sinless identity are diametrically opposed, so it's quite an adjustment to get into the swing of living as believers. Like acclimating to a new neighborhood or adapting to the culture at a new job, becoming comfortable with our identity as a new creation in Christ takes some getting used to. In fact, Galatians 6:15 affirms, "What counts is whether we have been transformed into a new creation." And we need just such affirmation to keep moving forward in the transformative growth that is shaping us into the vision God has for each of us.

Understanding identity is foundational because it is at work in many different ways in our society today. Our identities are being shaped by every message we receive. We internalize those messages, repeat them, and look for examples around us to affirm what we believe. But there's a higher, transcendent narrative (Christocentrism) that God intends for us to take in as our truth.

We all need to be affirmed. While on earth, even God the Son received affirmation from God the Father. At Jesus's baptism, God pointed out Jesus as our unique Savior. Luke 3:22 tells us that "the Holy Spirit, in bodily form, descended on him like a dove. And a voice from heaven said, 'You are my dearly loved Son, and you bring me great joy.'" Again, at the transfiguration, God set Jesus above two of the most important patriarchs of the faith:

> About eight days later Jesus took Peter, John, and James up on a mountain to pray. And as he was praying, the appearance of his face was transformed, and his clothes became dazzling white. Suddenly, two men, Moses and Elijah, appeared and began talking with Jesus. They were glorious to see. And they were speaking about his exodus from this world, which was about to be fulfilled in Jerusalem.
>
> Peter and the others had fallen asleep. When they woke up, they saw Jesus' glory and the two men standing with him. As Moses and Elijah were starting to leave, Peter, not even knowing what he was saying, blurted out, "Master, it's wonderful for us to be here! Let's make three shelters as memorials—one for you, one for Moses, and one for Elijah." But even as he was saying this, a cloud overshadowed them, and terror gripped them as the cloud covered them.
>
> Then a voice from the cloud said, "This is my Son, my Chosen One. Listen to him." When the voice finished, Jesus was there alone.
>
> Luke 9:28–36

## Cultural Identity

We see that even Jesus received affirmation, but what is the standard for it? How are we to relate to one another? We are not affirmed in a vacuum. The standard for affirmation must be above the one that identifies only based on culture. The Bible clearly speaks about the blessing found in unity.

> Behold, how good and how pleasant *it is*
> For brethren to dwell together in unity!
>
> *It is* like the precious oil upon the head,
> Running down on the beard,
> The beard of Aaron,
> Running down on the edge of his garments.
> *It is* like the dew of Hermon,
> Descending upon the mountains of Zion;
> For there the LORD commanded the blessing—
> Life forevermore.
>
> Psalm 133 NKJV

Understanding false identity is critical when it comes to who we allow to name us. To be named solely by our political affiliation, denomination, or race (or ethnicity) is to be identified with the stereotypes strongly held by and about those groups. It's crucial that our identity comes from God's mind and heart. We must allow our Father God to name us and always wear that name on top of all else.

It is possible to follow a culture rather than Jesus. Christian culture has tied itself to stuff that's not aligned with the Bible's perspective. Love of the world is why we're so divided in the faith from one another.

So how do we start down the road to change? As Einstein put it, "We have to learn to think in a new way."[1] Some have gone on to paraphrase this as "We cannot solve a problem by using the same level of thinking used to create it." Today, we might state it this way: To solve our cultural and racial divides, we need a new language. A language that is not rooted in the wisdom from beneath but the wisdom that comes from above.

We can start by identifying or naming ourselves as family with each other first. You see, identity is sneaky and subtle. We all have a part in shaping culture simply because we're present in it. We must look at ourselves first and ask, *How do I think about culture? Do I identify with God first?* And we must know that we will be held accountable for what God called us to do in regard to unity.

## Christ-Centered Community

Community affirms our new, Christ-centered identity. We were created to function in true community because life is a full-contact sport, face-to-face with fellow human beings in real-time.

I am blessed to come from a family that instilled a deep sense of belonging and identity in me. In my earlier days it was primarily about being a Welch. We are a very large and loving family and have a presence in our community that goes back four generations. The Welch family is the family that gets "adopted" by other individuals as their surrogate family. So, as you can imagine, this tends to spread out and cover a city pretty well. I always felt that I could go to any of my relatives' houses at any time and be welcomed with open arms. Yes, I'm blessed. Since my early identity was built on such strong, solid ground, I think it has been fairly easy for me to understand the importance of identity.

I knew who I was as a Welch, and when I became a follower of Jesus, I needed to delve into knowledge of my new identity. Becoming a Jesus-follower was and is the decision that changed my core—Skot Welch, a son of God whom God created African American, to be a father, husband, a son of Ruth Ann Welch and Fred Griffis—you get the picture. There are so many facets to my identity, but the most important facet is the only one that connects heaven to earth and that is Skot Welch, a son of God.

Everything else that I have been created to be—father, husband, African American, even a Welch—must bow its knee and comes after my relationship with Jesus.

My relationship with Christ—and with other Christians—is preeminent. I should look at and make decisions—every decision—from and through the lens of Christ first. It is this point of origin that helps make me more effective in all the other facets of life. I'm not saying this is easy, but kingdom prioritization brings a clarity that I believe makes other decisions somewhat easier.

The habit of sending every decision through the sieve of "what would Jesus do" is a process and a journey, but it is my prayer that every Christian would start this process and embark on this journey. If we as a community of believers pursued being what I call *Christocentric* Christians, a very clear and specific behavioral shift would follow, impacting our relationships with one another in communities, congregations, and families in a phenomenally positive way.

Ever since we became more conscious about this way of life, my wife, Barbara, and I have worked to instill this mindset into our children, who are young adults. My prayer is that they would go further faster in promoting and bringing about racial unity and understanding not just in the church but also in the marketplace, where God continues to increase their influence.

I was brought up in church. I was a pretty good kid, too, probably because my mom and my family were old-school in the area of discipline. I always knew that my aunts and uncles had the authority to offer correction when they felt it necessary, but because I was the first child born to the family and the oldest "big cousin," they rarely did. Yes, I was a bit spoiled. Still, values like discipline-by-village were solidly connected to and shaped by the church. My early years as a Christian were also shaped by some amazing and wonderful pastors and congregations—Pastor Lyman Parks Sr. of First Community A.M.E. Church (African Methodist Episcopal), who was also the first African American mayor of Grand Rapids,

Michigan, and Reverend Dr. Clifton Rhodes Jr. of Messiah Missionary Baptist Church. Even today, as I write this, I get pretty emotional when I think about these great men and the wonderful congregations they led for so many years.

These people of God loved me, always made time for me, and always made sure I knew how proud they were of me. That expectation, those continual votes of confidence, made me always strive against disappointing them or the people in the congregations who adopted me as their surrogate son or grandson. They expected great things of me, and by God's grace, I yearned to measure up. Even when I would mess up or do something I knew wasn't the right thing, as a maturing young person, I knew the expectation of others mattered a great deal. So when I faltered, the prayers, love, and confidence in me from adults around me helped me to get back up.

I believe this had everything to do with my coming to Christ. I was surrounded by the love of God through so many people—not perfect people, but incredibly generous and loving individuals.

During my formative years of eight to ten years old, I lived overseas with my mom and stepfather, Phillip Jones. My stepdad was in the army. He and my mom married not too long after they met, and before I knew it, we were headed overseas. Korea! What? I didn't even know what a "Korea" was. I just knew that I would be leaving my extended family, whom I adored with all of my heart.

But a time that could have been a lonely journey, a catastrophic blow to my confidence, turned into an incredible two years of growth immersion in this amazing and beautiful culture. Being thousands of miles away from all that was familiar, my parents made sure they created community for me as quickly as possible. Some of my stepdad's friends and my mom's friends quickly became family.

It occurred to me many years later that I was essentially homeschooled before *homeschooling* was cool. You see, my parents chose to live in the village with the local citizens instead of on the Camp Casey military base. My mom and stepdad would head to base every morning and leave me with our housekeeper and friend of the family, Gloria (not her Korean name).

Gloria tried her best to make sure I didn't get into too much trouble, and that worked most of the time; however, I was the *only* American kid in the village—not just the only African American kid. Being eight years old, I made friends with the village kids and learned just enough Korean to be dangerous. I also made friends with the folks at the local Tae Kwon Do school, restaurant, tailor shop, and so on.

Gloria took me everywhere she went and introduced me to the locals to make sure they knew who I was. She also put them on notice that they should watch out for me if she wasn't around. Community was happening. By the time I returned to the States, I was an adopted child of the village and knew my way around every nook and cranny of that small city. Even today, I consider Korea a part of my story of home.

That's just one example of how I took advantage of being an army brat. Having the opportunity to experience various societies and ethnicities gave me a strong taste for travel and for other cultures. And praise God, I've had the pleasure of going to many cities and countries around the world. (Wow, thank You, Lord, for my upbringing.) This isn't to claim, by any means, a perfect upbringing; no one has one of those. But it is to say that the environment in which I was brought up made my decision to follow Christ a fairly easy one.

Accepting Christ was like diving into another new culture, only this immersion has eternal significance and consequences. God will guide us in the area we're specifically called to. I've worked at the intersection of diversity, inclusion, and innovation for more than two decades, and I love it. I love people. I love the fact that we aren't the same. I love being in rooms where unity in God's mosaic is embraced.

## Don't Conform—Transform

Once we say we're born again, what happens after that? Most of us simply add the Christian label to all we've already been. That may be salvation, but it's not regeneration. Regeneration means we stop being what we used to be and start being the new person Christ molds us to be. Of course, all Christ wants us to be will not manifest at once, but we should be cooperating with the Spirit helping us to work that new person out. We will be going through the transformation until the day we die, and although we won't reach perfection, we can strive for excellence in our transformation.

There's a difference between a culture of excellence and one of perfection. Perfection focuses on what's wrong, the mistakes. Perfection sees five *A*'s and one *C*- on your child's report card and asks, "What's going on here? Why did you get that C-?" Excellence sees that same report card and says, "You are doing an amazing job. Look at these five *A*'s! I can tell you worked hard to get them. Did you try your best in this C- class? What help do you need to pull up that grade?" We honor people by celebrating all they are without tripping over what they are not. As humans, we are all in development. When there's a culture of excellence surrounding us, we thrive. In rooms with an atmosphere of perfection, we suffocate.

The man in the Bible at the pool of Bethesda lived in a community of the sick and was named by his sickness. Jesus showed up and asked him a simple question, "Do you want to be well?" His identity had so long been characterized by his sickness that he didn't know how to accept the excellence of health Jesus was able to give him.

Do we want to be well? Do we want to break from our community identity if that means stepping up to God's level? Just because we've made a mistake doesn't mean we *are* a mistake. Our mistakes, illnesses, etc. don't need to define us unless we want them to do so.

Feeling ashamed about a wrong we committed is not the same as being shamed. Many times, we don't know what we don't know. And we won't know what we don't know until we expose ourselves to those who are not like us.

## Victor Not Victim

As Christocentric Christians, our identity cannot be based on what our grandparents, parents, aunts, and uncles spoke into our lives unless what they said identically matched the Bible's dictates. In the Christian culture we've created, we often look to be persecuted. We've built walls and constructed a narrative that supersedes what God says. The Bible is a book about escape from bondage to freedom. The problems of our separation from each other cannot continue to be seen as larger than God Himself. The voice we most agree with is reflective of the idol that's already on the throne of our heart.

## Go on the Journey

We must elevate the way we think in order to be Christocentric Christians. We're going to prioritize affiliations, denominations, political parties, communities, social and ethnic identities, etc. while we explore how to be one. Just as our bodies have many parts and each part has a special function, so it is with Christ's body. We are many parts of one body, and we all belong to each other (Romans 12:4–5).

> The human body has many parts, but the many parts make up one whole body. So, it is with the body of Christ. Some of us are Jews, some are Gentiles, some are slaves, and some are free. But we have all been baptized into one body by one Spirit, and we all share the same Spirit.
>
> 1 Corinthians 12:12–13

And Jesus said it best:

> I pray that they will all be one, just as you and I are one—as you are in me, Father, and I am in you. And may they be in us so that the world will believe you sent me.
>
> John 17:21

Notice in the above verse that our unity as believers is not just what we say but what we actually do. It is what made Jesus's ministry attractive to those who didn't know Him. We must begin to think the way God thinks about unity and see false identities for what they are. God loves us too much to leave us blinded by lies.

Don't you find it interesting—actually alarming—that we can be so polarized while John 17:21, among other verses, clearly calls for unity among the Christian family? We call each other names and divide along political lines, denominational lines, and other lines we imagine and create. The division may satisfy our need for comfort, but division breaks God's heart. How can we overcome it?

## Closing the Fracture

1. In the time since becoming a Christ-follower, what culture have you continued to live in?
2. God says, "Wow," about everything He created, including the many cultures that exist.
   A. List three things about your culture of origin about which God has said "Wow."
   B. Now list three things about another culture about which God has said "Wow."
   C. Now list three things you and another culture have in common about which God can say "Wow."

3. In what ways have you seen yourself following culture more than you are following Jesus?
4. Do you want to be well? What scares you about becoming totally immersed in Christ culture?
5. Are you willing to transform?

## Glossary of Chapter Terms

**Ethnic**—Someone or something associated with a particular group that has a shared national origin or cultural identity.

**Racial**—Relating to the major groupings into which humankind is sometimes divided on the basis of physical characteristics or shared ancestry although "race" cannot be seen, as it is in actuality a socioeconomic construct. The concept of "race" was created by man.

**Diversity**—A combination of our differences that shape our view of the world, our perspective, and our approach. All the ways we are alike and respect for the ways that we are different.

**Racism**—"The assumption that psychocultural traits and capacities are determined by biological race and that races differ decisively from one another, which is usually coupled with a belief in the inherent superiority of a particular race and its right to domination over others."[2] Racism may also be defined as "prejudice, discrimination, or antagonism directed against other people because they are of a different race or ethnicity."[3]

**Culture**—Culture represents "the values, norms, and traditions that affect how individuals of a particular group perceive, think, interact, behave, and make judgments about their world."[4] Paraphrase: It's the way we do things. . . .

**Mosaic**—A decoration "made by inlaying small pieces of variously colored material to form pictures or patterns."[5] All God's people.

**Christocentric**—Having Christ as center; Christ-centered.

**Ethnocentric**—Having one's culture or ethnicity as center; culture-centered.

**Cultural Identity**—"Identification with, or sense of belonging to, a particular group based on various cultural categories, including nationality, ethnicity, gender, and religion."[6]

2

# Defeat Religious Racism

I believe the problem we're all dealing with is that we're all ethnocentric to some degree. And I believe that as Christians we are called to be Christocentric. Christ at the center. Christ is the One to whom we are to submit all we are. He is Lord. Really.

Sadly, the church is behind in the conversation about race. Since we say we're Christians, we're family no matter what color we are, so let's start this conversation by using the Bible—the family book. Let's lay down the politics, the denominations, and whatever else, not because they're not important, but because they should not be first. This is family talk that can get messy at times, so we need the book as our basis. The stakes are high, but there is no other option but to face the issue head on.

## White Church/Black Church

One of the ways division is clearly seen on a regular basis in the Christian world is the entire notion of—and our acceptance of—the thinking and history behind the terms *white* and *black*. What exactly are we talking about when we speak of the "white church" and "black church"? In 1963 Dr. Martin Luther King Jr. said, "We must face the fact that in America, the church is still the most segregated major institution in America. At 11:00 on Sunday morning when we stand and sing and Christ has no east or west, we stand at the most segregated hour in this nation."[1] Historically, we can't talk about this separation without talking about slavery—the importation of Africans to this nation for the purpose of slavery and then the "Christianizing" of them. (And here we go with a messy part, hold on!) It took violence to condition these enslaved people into a slavery mindset that was not theirs.

The slave catechism shows there was an agenda to get the enslaved people "saved" but at the same time conditioned to believe that God's intent was for them to be subjugated. The thought of these Christian slave masters (what an oxymoron) was that slaves were not fully human, yet they had souls that needed to be saved. Of course, this dichotomous train of thought makes no sense. How do you on the one hand treat these enslaved people as chattel—equal in value when lined up beside pigs—yet on Sundays tell them they have souls that need saving—but you cannot worship with us in our church? Yes, we have different denominations, but the reason the AME (African Methodist Episcopal) church exists is because African American people were not allowed to join the Episcopal church. Why do we have HBCUs (Historically Black Colleges and Universities)? Because black people weren't allowed to attend the universities white people were attending. "White church/black church" is fallen language because you can't find it in Scripture. We have so normalized this concept that we accept it as just the way things are and should be. While I understand there may be a need to identify various groups, terms are often used to speak about how *different* we are. Yes, we are different in culture, but we sometimes act like we're completely different species. We look at the differences as liabilities instead of as assets. Diversity, which is God's idea, is not a burden but a blessing.

For example, stereotypical views suggest that "white churches" are unfeeling because their worship services may be considered more quiet and staid. "Black churches" may be considered out of control because members of the congregation are "noisy and excitable" in church services. The thinking is that white church members see themselves as being respectful in their silence but see black congregants as primitive in their excitability. Black church members see themselves as expressing their praise while the white congregants are seen as not honoring God because of the silence. But let me flip this over on its head because these "boxes" are limiting. One can absolutely find just the opposite as well—a noisier white church and a quieter black church. God will never be put in a box.

These polar-opposite views and attitudes come across as though one group has a monopoly on the ways of God and on what God accepts as appropriate worship. Even if the stereotypes of quiet versus excitable are true, neither of these modes is better or worse; they are simply different. God created the generations, ethnicities, genders, and nationalities. The fact is that it is through the *diversity* in the body of Christ that we will be able to have a grasp of the awesomeness, beauty, and complexity of our God. Ephesians 3:17–19 (NASB, emphasis added) puts it like this:

> So that Christ may dwell in your hearts through faith; and that you, being rooted and grounded in love, may be able to comprehend *with all the saints* what is the breadth and length and height and depth, and to know the love of Christ which surpasses knowledge, that you may be filled up to all the fullness of God.

## Normal Is Not Normal

A conclusion is often where we stop thinking, and we have come to a conclusion now. We have stopped thinking because we've accepted the differences history has drawn between black and white Christians. However, just because we're used to something doesn't make that something right and acceptable. When we hold up where we are now and look through the Christocentric lens of Revelation 7:9; Psalm 133; John 17; and Ephesians 3:17, we can clearly see we are not healthy as a faith-based community. Our abnormality has become comfortable. If we can ultimately agree that God's ways are normal and our ways apart from Him are abnormal, we can start moving toward being a healthy church.

Relationship is everything. We like spending time with people who are similar to us. However, we must do life with people who are not like us if we ever plan to live as God intends. We are not experiencing unity simply by hanging out near people who are different until we find someone from "over there" who agrees with us. Extending ourselves into each other's lives until we start learning about the whys behind the differences is where true unity begins.

## Church Culture Appropriation

Eating food at a Chinese restaurant does not make us Chinese, yet in a similar fashion we are expecting people in our churches to move toward assimilation. Church culture appropriation happens when we seek to extract what we like from another culture while leaving the people of that culture group behind. For example, we say, "I like your music, bring that over to us, but don't bring me your concerns about the problems in the community where you live."

We only move toward fixing all of this if we listen, accept, and talk to each other. We cannot solve problems we don't acknowledge, and we cannot acknowledge problems we have never heard of. We're like the child with his hands over his ears screaming, "La la la la la," as his mother tells him what she wants him to hear. We are fearful of feeling guilty or victimized, but we must face whatever feelings may come if we intend to tackle these racial issues and turn toward unity. There is an unwillingness to change the status quo, and to be silent is to be complicit. Jesus is not going to lower the standard for us. We must come up to where He is in the conversation about unity. Perhaps if we become more anti-sin as opposed to being pro-comfort, we can start to grow.

We must get to the place where we understand that when Revelation 7:9 talks about every tribe, every nation, and every tongue, the picture is being painted of various languages all saying the same thing. There is true comfort—true unity—in being unified although not uniform.

## Cup Christianity

Division puts our immaturity as Christians on full display. Here's what I mean: Division and immaturity are two sides of the same coin, just as unity and maturity are two sides of another. The apostle Paul explained:

> Now I exhort you, brethren, by the name of our Lord Jesus Christ, that you all agree and that there be no divisions among you, but that you be made complete in the same mind and in the same judgment. For I have been informed concerning you, my brethren, by Chloe's people, that there are quarrels among you. Now I mean this, that each one of you is saying, "I am of Paul," and "I of Apollos," and "I of Cephas," and "I of Christ." Has Christ been divided? Paul was not crucified for you, was he? Or were you baptized in the name of Paul?
>
> 1 Corinthians 1:10–14 NASB

My answer is an emphatic NO!

My pastor, Joel A. Brooks Jr., calls this sort of immaturity "cup Christianity." There are Christians who will only accept something that supposedly increases their spiritual growth if it's in a certain kind of cup (a certain genre of music cup; a certain color of person cup; a certain kind of socioeconomic cup; a certain type of teaching or preaching style cup; a certain gender cup doing the teaching or preaching—generally a man; and even a certain political-stance cup).

But here's the deception: If one's focus is only on the cup, that means that it's all about the cup and not about the contents of the cup. In other words, a person could put any type of contents (bad teaching, false doctrine, bigotry, hatred, nationalism, and so on) in the cup but because the recipient is a cup-oriented Christian, they gulp the contents down without any reservation. Not healthy. And as Jesus said, a house divided against itself will fall: "Jesus knew their thoughts and said to them: 'Any kingdom divided against itself will be ruined, and a house divided against itself will fall'" (Luke 11:17 NIV).

We have the capacity to become so much better. First Corinthians 13 (NKJV) helps us to understand the connection between love and maturity:

> Though I speak with the tongues of men and of angels, but have not love, I have become sounding brass or a clanging cymbal. And though I have the gift of prophecy, and understand all mysteries and all knowledge, and though I have all faith, so that I could remove mountains, but have not love, I am nothing. And though I bestow all my goods to feed the poor, and though I give my body to be burned, but have not love, it profits me nothing.
>
> Love suffers long and is kind; love does not envy; love does not parade itself, is not puffed up; does not behave rudely, does not seek its own, is not provoked, thinks no evil; does not rejoice in iniquity, but rejoices in the truth; bears all things, believes all things, hopes all things, endures all things.
>
> Love never fails. But whether there are prophecies, they will fail; whether there are tongues, they will cease; whether there is knowledge, it will vanish away. For we know in part and we prophesy in part. But when that which is perfect has come, then that which is in part will be done away.

> When I was a child, I spoke as a child, I understood as a child, I thought as a child; but when I became a man, I put away childish things. For now we see in a mirror, dimly, but then face to face. Now I know in part, but then I shall know just as I also am known.
>
> And now abide faith, hope, love, these three; but the greatest of these is love.

So, let's use a hypothetical situation for the purpose of illustration. God designed a certain man with many facets. His ethnicity is African American, and that has driven and informed all of his decisions. His ethnicity determined who he spent his time with, made friends with, lived in community with, and worshiped with. He only went to places where African Americans went, and he only hired African Americans in his business. He only voted for candidates who looked like him. He knew the Word of God said to love his neighbor, but again, he qualified this commandment. He would only love the neighbor who looked like him, acted like him, thought like him, and agreed with him at all times. He knew God's Scriptures say, "If someone says, 'I love God,' but hates a fellow believer, that person is a liar; for if we don't love people we can see, how can we love God, whom we cannot see? And he has given us this command: Those who love God must also love their fellow believers" (1 John 4:20–21). Note that the biblical meaning of the Greek word translated "hate" here is to love less than someone or something else.

Here's the problem: Some of us reading the example will see nothing wrong when, actually, there are a number of things out of sync. Now, I am *not* saying that I don't love being around African Americans. Nor am I saying that I don't love my beautiful culture and heritage that predates the Middle Passage, and the Civil Rights Act of 1964. And I am not saying I am not proud of my legacy of coming from African kings and queens. What I *am* saying is that I cannot think like the hypothetical man in the scenario.

God's Word requires much more of me as it relates to fellow believers who don't look, think, or act like I do. God mandates that I live in community with those who are different from me. Why? Because diversity is God's idea, and He knows that we are smarter together than we are apart from one another. If my actions only aligned with my level of desired comfort and how "sameness" brought that comfort, then I have made my ethnicity an *idol* because I am placing my ethnicity above the authority that I give the Word of God in my life.

There are many studies that suggest we human beings naturally gravitate toward being with other people who are like us. Dr. Gwendolyn Seidman reported in *Psychology Today* on one such study that examined five proposed reasons for the link between similarity and liking. Some were pretty straightforward, such as a greater assurance of being liked: "We assume that someone who has a lot in common with us is more likely to like us. And in turn, we are more likely to like people if we think they like us."[2] The assumption of "fun and enjoyable interactions" among people who have things in common and the fact that "meeting people who share our attitudes makes us feel more confident in our own attitudes" also were considered.[3]

In what's termed "cognitive evaluation," learning we have something in common with an individual "makes us feel positively about that person, because we feel positively about ourselves" and we assume that, like us, that person has other good qualities too. And finally, people are more likely to perceive opportunities to gain new experiences and knowledge "when interacting with someone who is similar, rather than dissimilar, to them."[4]

Studies notwithstanding, although we may naturally gravitate toward and *like* people we judge to be similar to us in some way, that doesn't mean we have to *dislike* people who are different. If we dislike people just because they're different, we are idolizing similarity and promoting division.

## Religiosity and Racism

Brian McLaren wrote the article "The 'Alt-Right' Has Created Alt-Christianity" about the wickedness of racism attempting to wear a pious face. Consider those participating in the ultimately tragic series of events in 2017 in Charlottesville, Virginia, where not only did white racists spew pro-Hitler, anti-Jew, anti-black hate speech while espousing the "God-family-and-country" ideology and slogan, and head to a church service after the events that took place, but also where Heather Heyer was killed by James Alex Fields Jr., who drove his car into a crowd of counterprotesters. McLaren wrote:

> So as traditional Christian institutions shrink, stagnate and struggle [white nationalist and "alt-right" leader Richard] Spencer and his white-supremacist allies, feeling supported . . . , are creating a violent alt-Christianity, as their counterparts in the Middle East have created an alt-Islam. They are supplying their followers with alt-liturgies, alt-mysticism, and alt-magic and are willing to smash, burn, destroy and kill for it, as they idolize their vision of "America" as a white "ethno-state," an absolutized, divinized race and nation.[5]

Religiosity and racism go hand-in-hand. It is the *spirit* of religion—false Christianity—that causes a person to see other people as undesirable in this way. God had to break the apostle Peter from this false outlook. Listen in on the conversation between God and Peter:

> And I heard a voice saying to me, "Rise, Peter; kill and eat."
>
> But I said, "Not so, Lord! For nothing common or unclean has at any time entered my mouth." But the voice answered me again from heaven, "What God has cleansed you must not call common."
>
> Acts 11:7–9 NKJV

In his article "What is a Religious Spirit?," Curt Landry gives us greater insight into the insidious nature of the spirit of religion:

> A *religious spirit* is a type of demonic spirit that influences a person, or group of people, to replace a genuine relationship with God with works and traditions. When people operate out of a religious spirit, they attempt to earn salvation. This evil spirit has established nonbiblical beliefs and customs for generations. Yet, as Believers, we shouldn't turn a blind eye to the work of the religious spirit. It is lurking around attempting to cause judgment and destruction among Believers and in the Body of Church.[6]

We know the enemy appears as an angel of light, attempting to counterfeit any of God's good and perfect gifts, in efforts to cause chaos, confusion, shame, and guilt. He does this with the work of the religious spirit. "For such men are false apostles, deceitful workmen, masquerading as apostles of Christ. And no wonder, for Satan himself masquerades as an angel of light" (2 Corinthians 11:13–14 NIV).

This religious spirit is out to imitate the work of the Holy Spirit. We must be clear that no matter how hard Satan tries to forge the work of the Holy Spirit, he cannot. But he can cause great confusion and deception. The good news is this: When you are led by the Holy Spirit, you will be able to identify and deal with this bitter and hypocritical spirit.

## A Religious Spirit Is Bondage

As Peter Lucas Hulen, a professor at Wabash College, explains, "The Latin verb *religare* means to 're-bind.' The Latin noun *religio* referring to obligation, bond, or reverence is probably based on religare, so *religio* and its English derivation *religion* connote a 're-binding.'"[7] Hence, the root for the term *religion* is to bind. It is the spirit of religion that allowed the massacre of millions—

from slavery in the United States and other parts of the world, to apartheid in South Africa. Not only were certain religious denominations aware of this egregious activity of intentional brutality and bondage of certain ethnic groups but, in some instances, they affirmed the activity as being congruent with God's will. And even today, it is our silence—the silence of those who make up the church—that allows many of the recurrent tragedies, from Trayvon Martin to Sandra Bland, to Breonna Taylor, to Philando Castile, to George Floyd, to Patrick Lyoya, to name just a few. In an article entitled "The Curious Evangelical Silence over Trayvon Martin," writer Kimberly Davis states, "So far, the leading evangelical Christian leaders appear to be silent. And that silence is deafening."[8]

Repeatedly, black community pain, outrage, and resistance over these escalating killings have been met by the overall silence of the white evangelical community. These killings have taken place mostly without a word, even from often outspoken white evangelicals. What about the victims made them unworthy of compassion, outrage, or speaking out? *She had a police record. He was selling untaxed cigarettes. He had a busted taillight. He was reported to have had a weapon. She resisted arrest. He was running from the police.* The excuses are varied, but no less painful.

None of those individuals, who happened to be African American, should have died with the church standing silent and simply calling it a "black problem." What Dr. Martin Luther King Jr. addressed in his "Letter from a Birmingham Jail" has persisted over recent decades:

> Wherever the early Christians entered a town the power structure got disturbed and immediately sought to convict them for being "disturbers of the peace" and "outside agitators." But they went on with the conviction that they were a "colony of heaven," and had to obey God rather than man. They were small in number but big in commitment. They were too God-intoxicated to be "astronomically

> intimidated." They brought an end to such ancient evils as infanticide and gladiatorial contest.
>
> Things are different now. The contemporary church is often a weak, ineffectual voice with an uncertain sound. It is so often the arch-supporter of the status quo. Far from being disturbed by the presence of the church, the power structure of the average community is consoled by the church's silent and often vocal sanction of things as they are.[9]

In other words, we the people, who make up the church, have been quick to pass the buck and are generally silent when it comes to matters that might be considered controversial. Are we or aren't we a multiethnic family? God says we are and didn't ask us for our opinion. In all of the aforementioned instances, and there are many more, injustice built upon the foundation of years of inequity is at the root. The Bible says plainly that not only is justice important to God, but the very foundation of God's throne rests upon it: "Righteousness and justice are the foundation of your throne. Unfailing love and truth walk before you as attendants" (Psalm 89:14).

So, if justice is so fundamental to the very nature of God, the One who created us, isn't it elementary to believe that it should be manifested in the life of every Christian, regardless of denomination, political party, or ethnicity? The only way we can dismiss this spiritual imperative is to ultimately put ourselves in opposition to God.

One of the awesome things about God is the grace we receive to repent and to change. Grace is not provided to enable us to continue in our error but to change our thinking, turn from the wrong way, and go the right way. We must move from our self-centered, idolatrous manner of operating to a God-centered way of thinking and living. This is what we will call throughout this book a *Christ-centered, ethnic-conscious (Christocentric ethnoconscious) identity*. And this is not to be confused with an *ethnic-centered,*

*Christ-conscious (ethnocentric Christoconscious)* identity. The difference between the identifications is as far as the east is from the west. Let's define the terms: The definitions of word parts are as follows:

*Christo*—Anything pertaining to Jesus Christ
*Ethno*—Having to do with one's people group or ethnicity
*Centric*—Revolving around, having at the center
Conscious—Having knowledge of something; aware.

Let's go deeper:

1. *Ethnocentrism*—Evaluation of other cultures according to preconceptions originating in the standards and customs of one's own culture.
2. *Christocentrism*—Having Christ as its center; Christ-centered
3. *Ethnoconscious*—Being aware of one's own people group
4. *Christoconscious*—Having knowledge of or being aware of Christ

## A Christocentric Ethnoconscious Life versus an Ethnocentric Christoconscious Life

Let's go a little deeper still. Here's the thing: God loves all humans—those made in God's image—the same. God loves the skin we're in. God loves the people group we come from, our nationality, and our hair texture. God loves all the stuff that makes us *us*. God loves the stuff God created and put in us before the foundation of the world. God has no problem with any of it because God created it. God does, however, have a problem with those things when they become preeminent or dominant over Lordship of God's Son Jesus in our lives.

So let's look more closely at the differences between the *cultural* Christian and the *covenant* Christian. The cultural Christian is weak and carnal; living the ethnocentric Christoconscious life puts us in a place of nonresistance to winds of popular opinion but ultimately leaves a person spiritually empty, which in turn leaves them open to anything—whether it reflects the nature of God or not. The covenant Christian is strong and spiritual; living the Christocentric ethnoconscious life gives Jesus His rightful place on the throne of our heart while also providing us with a greater sense and appreciation for who He made us, without apology. This is a place of strength. The Lord made me an African American—this is not a mistake. Furthermore, He didn't put me on the earth to live a life of struggle, marginalization, or victimhood but one of victory and joy. I don't have to spend my life looking for approval, and the reason for that is simple: It's because I come *from* approval.

How do you think it feels for African Americans to look around and hear the silence of those who are supposed to be Christian allies? How do black Christians re-enter their sanctuaries and offices with white Christians after the election of a black president or a George Floyd-type incident? A black person can feel not only unsupported but invisible when kingdom family members stay completely detached. Society fills the vacuum left by the silence. Real biblical unity demands maturity. Black Christians, white Christians must obey God rather than man.

When God says, "Unify," we must remember that His Word has already given us the grace, ability, and power to bring unification to pass. We can do what He commands us to do. It's time to get busy as the family of God.

## Closing the Fracture

1. How would you define a white church?
2. How would you define a black church?

3. Based upon your definitions above, explain how the Bible justifies those definitions.
4. What things are in your "cup" that you can start loosening your grip on for the sake of unity?
5. Choose a racially charged incident that has happened recently. Have a listening time with a person of a different ethnicity and listen to his or her viewpoint and feelings.
6. What do you understand about Christoconsciousness and ethnoconsciousness?

## Glossary of Chapter Terms

**Cultural Appropriation**—"The unacknowledged or inappropriate adoption of the customs, practices, ideas, etc. of one people or society by members of another and typically more dominant people or society."[10]

**Cup Christianity**—Coined by Pastor Joel A. Brooks Jr., the label refers to a form of "Christianity" rooted in particular ethnic cultural traditions—including music genre, preaching style, worship style, or political or denominational affiliation—that cause the receiver of the tradition to accept or reject a tradition, concept, or even a group of people based upon its alignment with their preferred cultural tradition.

**Middle Passage**—The journey of captured Africans "lasted roughly 80 days on ships ranging from small schooners to massive, purpose-built 'slave ships.' Ship crews packed humans together on or below decks without space to sit up or move around. Without ventilation or sufficient water, about 15% grew sick and died."[11]

**Civil Rights Act of 1964**—Public Law 88–352 (78 Stat. 241) "prohibits discrimination on the basis of race, color, religion, sex or national origin." Its provisions forbade discrimination on the basis of sex and race "in hiring, promoting, and firing."[12]

**Idol**—An image or representation of a god used as an object of worship; something a person needs seek permission from before they do God's will.

**Christoconsciousness**—Knowledge of or awareness of Christ.

**Ethnoconsciousness**—Awareness of one's own people group.

# Examine Black Culture

Before we examine black culture as this chapter title suggests, we need to first lay a groundwork about why discussing this is important to our conversation. Two idols exist that must be destroyed, as Moses did with the golden calf. One is the myth and idol of white superiority; the other is the myth and idol of black inferiority. Just as white people must stop operating from an I-start-out-inherently-better-than-you mindset, black people must learn to operate from a mindset that understands themselves as exceptional, beautiful, and being born into a life that—made in the image of God—is not and cannot be defined by struggle, deficits, or "less-than," These mindsets must not be replaced, however, with idols of black superiority and white inferiority. And while many Christians among all persuasions ditched these idols long ago, striving with varying degrees of success to live their lives and their faith accordingly—reaching across divisions interpersonally, politically, and professionally, seeking out or developing multicultural and multiethnic churches, forming partnerships with congregations of other ethnicities, and so on—this side of heaven there will be work to do.

The covenant culture is to quit rehearsing the narrative of struggle. We don't forget about the horrors or the lingering effects of slavery, but we approach those truths knowing that both black and white have now and always have had the same covenant relationship with God. This understanding forever denies any people group the opportunity to define or determine the destiny of any other people group. Thinking about myself and anybody else on the planet as God thinks about us radically changes the internal narrative.

## Covenant Christianity

Cultural Christians operate by evaluating other cultures through the lens of the standards and customs of their own culture, putting those preconceived notions ahead of whatever Christ would have to say. They know of Christ, that is they have Christ-consciousness, but they do not allow the words of Christ to permeate their experience to effect a change in their thoughts and beliefs. Since they base their beliefs about other cultures on what society has taught them (ethnocentricity) rather than on Christ, they put Christ's directives second. This results in these individuals living a weak life spiritually because one can only be strong spiritually if Christ is allowed to influence one's beliefs, thoughts, and actions.

So how do we realize God's mandate?

In an effort to consistently function as strong and spiritual covenant Christians who are living the Christocentric ethnoconscious life, it's essential that we have an understanding of cultures that are different from ours. That's what *ethnoconsciousness* is. The idea is not that we have to adopt everyone else's culture when it comes to how we "do church" and relate to God; the idea is that we come to an understanding of how others experience God and celebrate those cultures' expressions. It may well happen that we will learn of some expressions that we will then wish to adopt and include in our own worship experience, thus expanding and enriching our overall experience with God.

## Cultural Christianity Unifies

We can function as Christians no matter what color we are by simply understanding that different is not better or worse or right or wrong. Different is simply different. We can appreciate how each worships the God of the universe. This appreciation is not achieved through colorblindness—colorblindness is a liability, not an asset. We enjoyed black-and-white television only because we had never seen color TV. Once we saw color TV, black-and-white sets became obsolete. It will be the same with living together in unity as believers. There is power in multiethnic relationships in the faith community. Once we truly experience Christocentric-ethnoconsciousness, we'll never go back to being separatist in the faith again.

Once our eyes are open, we cannot stop seeing how entrenched racism is in our culture. It will cost us something to live as someone changed: apathy. Christianity, by nature, is for justice and against injustice.

## Be Bold and Transformed by Community

Don't try to make others feel comfortable in the face of racial inequity and injustice. Our white brothers and sisters must step up to be bold and not hitch their wagons to just one convenient side of the spectrum. For example, if life inside the womb is precious, all life outside of the womb (no matter what color) is precious as well. (And for *all* brothers and sisters who care about inequity and injustice facing people outside the womb, shouldn't there be concern for those inside of it?) Don't end up on the wrong side of justice.

As a people, we have a unique gift of separating from each other—in America, it's race/ethnicity against race/ethnicity; in Africa, it's bias from one tribe against another; in India, it's by caste, and in many countries, by class. Everywhere it's stupid. God knows we are transformed by our interactions with each other. This is why the enemy wants us to separate.

There are cultural levelers. Food, for example, can bring us together. Breaking bread together is all through Scripture. We appreciate each other by sharing history over our meals. When we come together in the kitchen, we experience each other as humans and are transformed by our contact with each other. Being a covenant Christian is similar to treating the church like a kitchen on a cooking show. So now, what is the African American worship experience like?

## The African American Worship Experience

The African American worship experience involves an understanding of a relationship with God that is as real as our relationships with physical family members. While discussing this chapter with one of my African American friends, she related the following story that begins to explain facets of black church culture:

> I work at a school that is sponsored by a conservative denomination peopled by mostly white congregants. We tease a lot about the difference between their worship service and my Baptist one. They note that they are in and out of church in just one hour, so they chide me about spending so much time in a church service, and about making so much noise. Meanwhile, I nickname them "the frozen chosen" and tell them that we're in church so long because we really like spending time with God. Despite the quips, some friends took me up on my invitation to visit my church one Sunday.
>
> They arrived (we'll call them Peter and Lilian) and brought their unchurched cousin along who was living with them at the

> time. My church is truly a black church with only two or three congregants of different ethnicities, so my friends were immediately noticed as visitors. They were greeted warmly and directed to prime seats by the ushers. Since I am one of the ministers on staff, I sit in the pulpit so I can see what's going on in the pews during the service. My friends participated as we stood and sang passionately throughout praise and worship time. They experienced the clapping and enjoyment of the choir, the enthusiasm expressed at offering time, fervent delivery of the sermon, and the eager anticipation of the invitation to accept Christ as Savior. They even stood when it was asked that visitors stand to be welcomed.
>
> After the service, I was eager to hear their reflections. Peter said, "The music was as amazing as I expected, but I was unprepared to hear the congregation singing so well. Everybody around me could sing too!" He also commented that having the men (the deacons) go up front first to give their money at offering time was a great idea showing a positive example to the young people.
>
> Lilian added that she had asked her cousin what she thought of the service, and the evaluation from someone who was not familiar with church of any kind was spot-on. The cousin observed, "This service was like a big pep rally for Jesus."

Lilian's cousin had perceived the essence of the black church experience in terms of what she knew. "Pep rallies" whip the fans into a frenzy around the exploits of the team and the main champion. At pep rallies, fans dress in the team colors, shout accolades to the team, enthusiastically praise the champions' extraordinary feats, and share in team victories and defeats. In the end, true fans remain loyal, having faith in the team and the champion no matter what the outcome of that particular game, match, or contest. Fans trust the coach, maintain belief in the champion, and swear allegiance to the team, always knowing that no matter the present state of affairs, there's a brighter day ahead.

All the characteristics voiced by the visitors after attending just one service at my friend's church have their roots deeply embedded in black culture. These roots are not there to be dug up and destroyed, but to be understood and celebrated. At the same time, these roots must be submitted to their place at Jesus's feet, not idolized above God. White people can come to understand and respect the black cultural church experience, and black people can loosen their grip on the same cultural church experience by understanding that their way of worship, although a comfortable, enjoyable pattern, is not a biblical mandate. So let's look more closely at the origins of black culture as it relates to the African American church experience. To appreciate this experience, it is essential to discuss the preacher and preaching, the forms of music, and the styles of worship. Once these are explored, it will be clear how these forms can become idols of black church culture.

## The Preacher and Preaching

When it comes to the black preacher, his or her importance to the church and to the black community in America can be traced to before the end of the Civil War and the abolition of slavery. Once emancipated, though technically free, black people had little else beside their tenuous "freedom." The main thing black people had of their own was the church, and the preacher was the leader of the church. The preacher's stances, opinions (usually *his*), and guidance are held in high esteem in the black community. Through Reconstruction, the aftermath of Reconstruction, and the Jim Crow era of the South, African American preachers were looked up to as primary leaders in the community. The civil rights movement of the 1960s was largely organized, galvanized, and led by black preachers and pastors like Dr. Martin Luther King Jr. and others. As to black preaching, it had the dubious charge of walking the line between explaining biblical truth and exposing secular reality in a way that taught and encouraged a people who had basically been beat up all week. Preaching had to stay just this side of too much emotionalism but swing not too far away from touching the emotions needed to reassure blacks to "keep on keeping on," to embolden them to "fight the good fight." Cleophus LaRue, in his book *The Heart of Black Preaching*, lists the characteristics of African American preaching as "strong biblical content," "creative uses of language," "appeal to emotions," and "ministerial authority."[1] And Dr. R. Clifford Jones, in a 2002 *Ministry* magazine article, explains that "the primary objective of African-American preaching is to enable the listener to experience the grace and love of Jesus Christ, the response to which is usually one of celebration and praise," citing Frank A. Thomas's book, *They Like to Never Quit Praisin' God*.[2]

Black preaching originates with God and resonates with the people in a double-sided dialogue. One side consists of the preacher talking with God about what God wants the preacher to communicate to the people. The other side consists of the preacher talking with the people and the people talking back. Throughout the sermon, the preacher guides the dialogue by asking the congregation questions, such as "Can I get a witness?" and "Won't He do it?" The people respond—sometimes without the questions even being asked—with "amen," "hallelujah," and exclamations like "Preach it, preacher!" and "Say on, sir," or "Tell the truth; shame the devil!"

According to Dr. Jones, now dean of the School of Theology at Oakwood University,

> The cross of Christ is ever the substance and sum of Black preaching. . . .
>
> African-American preaching is at its best when it is undergirded by two important hermeneutical principles. The first is that the gospel must be declared in the language of the people. The second is that the gospel must scratch where the people itch.[3]

The statement is often heard among African American churchgoers that they "wouldn't have a God they couldn't feel sometimes." That means having the passion of the preaching and the rest of the worship experience or it's not worth spending the time at church.

While I understand the quest for emotional connection with God, sometimes the excitement may disguise or hide the issues we don't want to have to work through. The *excitement* of the message can deflect attention from the *words* of the message that really need to be heard. We need to attend to the message about the change we need to make, the person we need to forgive, or that which we must submit to the Lord. This preaching style cannot be held up as an idol, obstructing our view of the real God and jamming the signals so we can no longer hear what "thus says the Lord."

God can also be heard in tranquility and in a still small voice.

## Forms of Music

There is no black church without African American *gospel* music. It is widely known that the early music of the African American church was an incredible mix of African drumbeats and rhythms as well as slavery's melancholy yet hopeful messages in freedom choruses; civil rights movement determination songs later came along, and the music has evolved so wonderfully into other powerful genres such as hip-hop and other contemporary sounds. Gospel music is as much about the black individual's relationship with God as it is about current life situations—again, a testament to the inextricable mix of the two. The understanding is that one cannot divorce a relationship with God from living everyday life.

For example, as enslaved Africans sang "Go Down Moses," they looked to the patriarch's story as a model for the escape from their plight. But they also coupled that chorus with "There's a

Meetin' Here Tonight," to signal that Harriet Tubman, a "Moses of her People," would be conducting the Underground Railroad through the plantation, picking up passengers to help them escape to their Promised Land. And as the words "I Will Trust in the Lord 'Til I Die" were sung from the pews, they were followed by the defiant choruses of "Ain't Gonna Let Nobody Turn Me 'Round," and "We Shall Overcome," from hearts emboldened by faith that God was on their side. Now we can hear African Americans keeping up the gospel music tradition singing about the God of their experience through earlier songs from the gospel musical revolution, like Kirk Franklin's "Stomp," which crossed over to be played on secular radio stations, to my dear friend and Grand Rapids native Pastor Marvin Sapp's global anthem, "Never Would Have Made It." These songs carry the message that, having endured difficult times, we will praise God wherever and whenever we please because without Him we would not have made it this far. And to experience a more current representation of the African American Christian church through music, you would have to immerse yourself in almost any and every genre of music that exists—"gospel jazz," rock, folk, experimental, and even EDM (electronic dance music). There is African American representation in all of these genres giving glory to God and pointing to Jesus as the way to salvation.

Even as we see that the African American musical experience is much more than volume and rhythm, we still dare not let it become an idol. In the same way preaching can become so, music can as well. Those preferring black gospel music over any other kind of Christian music are in danger of practicing, as mentioned earlier, cup Christianity. Granted, there is a rich heritage in the African American gospel music experience. However, we must not allow ourselves to hold the arrogant belief that the heritage of music from other cultures is not as rich and powerful.

Scores of diverse hymns detail the Bible's message beautifully. Pick up a hymnal and read through all the verses of the hymn writers. An amazing storehouse of finely worded truth from Scripture is housed there. Let us please not forget these treasures, such as "How Great Thou Art," based on a Swedish traditional melody and a poem written by Carl Boberg in Monsteras, Sweden in 1885. It was translated into German, then Russian, then finally into English by English missionary Stuart K. Hine, who added two original verses of his own. Also remember the great hymn "A Mighty Fortress is Our God" by the German reformer Martin Luther. These men were not African American, yet the hymns cannot be discounted because they are absent the rhythm of black ancestors.

## Forms of Worship

As Dr. R. Clifford Jones points out, three main things that happen in an African American worship experience are prayer, music, and preaching. There is always a celebratory aspect to any black church gathering, be it a church service, a concert, or even a funeral. Black people have learned to meet with God and simply be thankful for the Almighty allowing us "Another Day's Journey." Dr. Jones explains,

> For a people still facing daunting challenges, for many waking up "clothed in your right mind and experiencing a measure of health and strength" is reason enough to praise God that things are as good as they are. In African-American worship people have a good time in the Lord, and it is not uncommon as they leave a service to hear them ask: "Didn't we have church today?!" Yet to have church is not simply to engage in hand clapping, but to experience anew the liberating presence and power of Jesus Christ.[4]

Yes, the black church worship experience today rests on a rich heritage African Americans are proud to sustain. Yet, as African Americans fought hard to erase color lines in baseball, industry, and politics, will we fight as hard to erase color lines in the church? The only color that should count in the church is the red of Christ's blood, which unites us all. Will we examine our hearts around these issues of culture—black and white and other? Whatever the color of the leadership, I believe God expects to see the mosaic even in churches led by African Americans. While we are looking at and demanding more ethnic diversity within white-led churches, we must look at ourselves and ask what God is requiring of us as the Christians He created African American. His Word carries the same standard for us all.

## Closing the Fracture

1. Define "covenant Christianity" as you understand it from the beginning of this chapter.
2. Think about specific outlooks you hold about ethnicities other than your own. What changes will you have to make to be a covenant Christian?
3. After reading this chapter, what did you learn, and what can you appreciate about black preachers and black preaching?
4. After reading this chapter, what did you learn and what can you appreciate about black church music?
5. If you are white and you don't already do so, attend a church where most of the members are black or, at a minimum, people of color. Keep in mind what you learned in this chapter and then discuss your experience with a black friend and with white friends.
6. If you are black and you attend a church where the congregation is predominantly black, ask your pastor what's being done to make your church a place of belonging also for white people.

## Glossary of Chapter Terms

**Covenant Christianity**—Christianity that is based upon the belief that God's Word supersedes any and all man-made traditions, regardless of comfort, what other people think, or what one feels like doing. It particularly transcends ethnicity, political affiliation, denominational affiliation, and socioeconomic groups.

# Unveil White Culture

This chapter addresses the pervasiveness of white culture not as a negative, but as a framework by which we see things. In America, white culture is the default culture. Every other cultural celebration of church is then judged in terms of how similar it is to—or different from—what white culture deems as normal or right. So, the discussion to unveil white culture as it pertains to our current conversation is much different from the conversation of the former chapter. Black preaching and black music had to be explained because they are judged by the "standard" of what's acceptable by the default white church culture. It is just assumed that white preaching and white music do not have to be explained because they are already understood as the standard. Whether that's right or wrong is not the question; we're simply acknowledging that it is what it is. What we must explore here, if we ever plan to be unfractured, is the reality of this default. And why, you may ask, is this a problem to begin with? The problem is that when any group or person is at the center other than Christ,

His kingdom, and the unified family of God, idolatry will be the result of that ethnocentricity. And with that comes all sorts of fruit that positions people who don't fit that tradition as other, less than, not normal, and not like us (whoever *us* is).

Exactly what does the term *white* mean when it comes to people's identities? And when we refer to the *white church*, what does that mean? Does this emphasize the stratification, distinction, or the separation between people? Does it mean segregation?

In terms of the culture of the white church, many of these churches forbade African Americans from being members or even attending service in their congregations. A few denominations even had what they called "colored branches," a distinction that did not come from the churches led by people of color. The separation came because of the exclusion of African Americans from white-led congregations.

A case in point is the formation of the first African American denomination in the United States, the African Methodist Episcopal Church (AME), which "unlike most other American denominations, was formed because of racial issues rather than theological differences."

> The AME Church developed from a congregation formed by a group of Black people who withdrew in 1787 from St. George's Methodist Episcopal Church in Philadelphia because of restrictions in seating; Blacks had been confined to the gallery of the church. Those who withdrew formed the Free African Society, the forerunner of the AME Church, and built Bethel African Methodist Church in Philadelphia.[1]

Here is another example, occurring more than a century later in the Midwest:

> On September 13, 1907, the Michigan Annual Conference of the Methodist Episcopal Church voted against ordaining black

> bishops. The vote denied Black clergy leadership positions even within predominantly Black congregations. Delegates expressed concern that Black bishops may eventually lead white congregations and claimed that the moral inferiority of Black people required Black preachers to submit to white spiritual leadership.[2]

Thus, when we use the terms *white church* and *black church* we are using language that truly hearkens back to an earlier time when the owner of the local restaurant could be a deacon or elder in a church—and then forbid African Americans to sit at the counters of his restaurant.

## Let's Talk about Race

The word *race* as it refers to different people groups is only correctly used if referring to *the human race*. There is only one race. However, many of us find it hard to replace the old dead word *race*. While we will find Bible mentions of *ethnos* (nation), from which we get the word *ethnicity*, the word *race* is not used in original versions of Scripture other than when alluding to a person running one (see Psalm 19:5; Ecclesiastes 9:11; 1 Corinthians 9:24; Hebrews 12:1).

Why is this? It's because although *racism* is real, the concept of *race* is an invented one. Subdivisions of humankind have been proposed over the centuries, including efforts by French physician, traveler, and philosopher Francois Bernier in 1684[3] and Swedish botanist Carolus Linnaeus in 1735.[4] Then Johann Friedrich Blumenbach, a German anthropologist, physiologist, and comparative anatomist, divided humans into the five "varieties" published in his 1795 volume *On the Natural Variety of Mankind* and simplified below:

- ***Caucasian** (later known as the white race),* including peoples of European origin

- ***Mongolian*** *(yellow race)*, including all East Asians and some Central Asians
- ***Malayan*** *(brown race)*, including Southeast Asian and Pacific Islanders
- ***Ethiopian*** *(black race)*, including sub-Saharan Africans
- ***American*** *(red race)*, including American Indians[5]

Blumenbach's categorization of varieties (later races), with Caucasians as central, is the one that, with variations along the way, eventually became widely accepted and found its way into our lexicon. We use the language of race in everything from the US Census to job applications, to church services, even though "the consensus after the Second World War [is] that race is a social construct with minor biological components."[6]

Although racism is very real, *you cannot see race* because it is a socioeconomic construct that has no basis in science. There is no white race. There is no black race. The concept of race was created to stratify people and ultimately became the method by which people were and are discriminated against based on the concentration of brownness or melanin in the skin. Rooted in these ideologies, there is the white church culture. Let's get more specific about what's different about the white church. While each church body is different, there are some similarities, just as we examined with the black church culture. But this again is where God's mosaic expresses its beauty. He made us different for a reason. Sure, we all have preferences, which I address in what follows, but it is also important for us to walk in a higher level of maturity if, for example, the sound is not what we like traditionally. In the previous chapter I articulated for you the beauty of what society calls the black church. But just as unique and as beautiful is that which culture calls the white church. Even as I write this, I am still in conflict with the terms *white church* and *black church*, but I believe the illustration helps us land on the concept more quickly.

## Music

There can be a certain sound that gets tagged as "white Christian music" more so than other genres, and it often begins and ends with an acoustic guitar of some sort. And when things get a little loud, it usually ends up in a place of three to four chords, big drums, and a rock-and-roll or even alternative music feel. We're not at all deciding if this is bad or good; it's just different. All Christians can make room in our repertoire for the musical diversity and imagination of God.

While I will talk about a negative experience my family and I had, I think it's only fair to also say that my family and I have been members of congregations where our white brothers and sisters were in the majority, and I consider them as much a part of my family, and our family as much a part of theirs. The worship, the teaching, the music—all of it God used and continues to use to enrich my life. I have a musical background, so I appreciate all kinds of music and have taught my kids to do the same. To me, whether loud or soft, guitar- or keyboard-based, as long as I have an experience with God, with the presence of the Lord, that is all that matters.

I was actually one of the lead vocalists on the worship team of a predominantly white congregation of about 3,000. And I can say that the music we ministered—the time spent to pursue excellence in ways that would cause the presence of God to touch the lives of all who attended—are experiences I wouldn't trade for anything. I think that experience has everything to do with the ease with which I am able to move from genre to genre. I'm not after the genre—I'm after the God behind the genre. And I believe such is also the case for my white brothers and sisters who set the table every time the family of God gathers.

It is this lived experience that makes the story I am about to share such an odd one. So here goes:

My wife and I were in Washington, DC, and attended a church service with our daughter, in a neighborhood known as the Shaw

District. This district sits just down the hill from the world-renowned Howard University, a Historically Black College/University (HBCU). It's an educational institution that has produced some of the most impactful leaders of our time: Supreme Court Justice Thurgood Marshall, US Congressman Elijah Cummings, acclaimed actress Phylicia Rashad, Nobel literary laureate Toni Morrison, civil rights icon Andrew Young, Harlem Renaissance writer and filmmaker Zora Neale Hurston, and our current Vice President, Kamala Harris—to name a few. It is also the university from which my wife and son graduated, and our daughter was a senior there at this writing. Many call Howard "The Mecca."

Set one foot on Howard's campus and you know that you are someplace special, an area in the city of our nation's capital where African American intellectualism and culture thrive. During Howard's homecoming, where some 50,000-plus people have converged annually, our daughter asked us to go with her to the church she had been attending on a regular basis. We enthusiastically agreed, as we wholeheartedly encourage her and her brother to grow in their relationship with God. So that Sunday morning we met our daughter and a few of her friends in front of the theater where the church service was being held.

In this historically African American neighborhood, group upon group of white millennials congregated outside the theater with some numbering twenty or more, but with almost no people of color. I was concerned but thought, *I'm sure that it will get better*. People who were obviously on the hospitality committee, who I thought were there to greet visitors, simply stared at me and my family. We smiled at them; they looked at us and turned away. This happened no less than three times. It felt weird. I didn't want to say anything to my daughter because I didn't want to hurt her feelings (although we did speak about it in depth at brunch after the service—and she agreed).

We walked into the service, in the neighborhood where The Mecca is alive and well, and the service began. It was one of the whitest, most Eurocentric services I've ever experienced. From the staff to the musicians to the leadership to the vast majority of the congregants—virtually no people of color. And no African Americans of any number to make a visible difference. It was troubling. The service incorporated not a single element that said to anybody other than the white congregants, "We see you." Yet the service continued as though this was okay. Normal. The immersion in the culture of white was to such a degree it was difficult for me to hear the sermon, though the pastor was actually a very good teacher.

The overwhelming message we received: *This is the culture of* our *congregation. It's our music, our leadership, our way of modeling hospitality, our way of singing, and our way of being. Even though we are just down the hill from one of the preeminent institutions of higher learning on the planet that happens to be African American, in one of the most culturally diverse neighborhoods on the planet.*

I imagined a portrait of a blond-haired, blue-eyed Jesus nearby. Without saying a word, the clear message was received: *We offer no flexibility or any acknowledgment that any other ethnic culture than our own is important. This is the template, and we have no desire to deviate in any way to make you feel like you belong. No, you are merely welcome. Assimilate or move on.*

I know this observation sounds harsh. Yet the juxtaposition of the service we experienced and the neighborhood in which we had that experience was a little overwhelming. I even had the opportunity to meet the pastor after service but made no mention of all of the things going through my mind and heart, as I wanted to try to stay focused on the positive. My family did, however, have a great conversation with our daughter and a couple of her friends after the service as we got a bite to eat.

It was quite bothersome to hear that much of their time spent in their small groups, which I thought had the primary purpose of helping believers grow in their relationship with Jesus, had been spent answering "cultural questions" about ethnicity and the African American experience instead of being focused on the Word. This is ethnocentrism and Christo-consciousness. And I, like many African Americans who have experienced this, simply vote with our feet and never, unless the Lord says otherwise, attend another service such as this. Because there are alternatives.

Again, as I mentioned at the beginning of this section, this experience was the exception and not the rule. I think that's why it stood out so clearly to me—it was contrary to my other lived experience when my family and I were members of a predominantly white congregation.

## The White Church Triumphs

There is what church experts describe as the "triumphal" nature of white church culture. The preaching on grace is often so dominant that it never seems to dig into deeper discussion about sin rooted in racism, prejudice, bigotry, or injustice. In 2020, people from all around the globe experienced a brutal main street lynching that took the life of a man named George Floyd. He was murdered. Period. This public homicide was so obvious, so demonic, and so heartless that it caused people of all ethnicities all over the world to take to the streets to protest the killing of this man, alleged to have passed a counterfeit twenty-dollar bill in a convenience store. Nothing remotely worthy of his life being taken.

And yet, even in all of this, it seemed that white leaders hesitated in being vocal in a way that would cost them something. There were, however, some who did, including Senior Teaching Pastor Jeff Manion of Ada Bible Church in Grand Rapids Michigan.

At the time of the George Floyd murder, Ada Bible was involved in a series about the book of Proverbs. Unable to keep quiet, Manion paused the series to lead the multi-campus congregation into uncharted territory for their predominantly white congregation: taking a deep multi-week look at toxicity of societal injustice, racism, and prejudice, and challenge the congregation to act, take it personally, and learn the history of what led to this horrific point. And why it is the Christian's duty to both care and get involved.

He did it with grace, clarity, and strong conviction. It was refreshing, to say the least.

Just a couple states over, in downtown Minneapolis, Minnesota, where Floyd's life was taken, is my dear friend and former pastor Scott Hagan, who at the time was president of North Central University (NCU). North Central is a university committed to creating a learning environment where the value of God's mosaic of individuals is woven into every aspect of curriculum and its operations. It is also noteworthy that it was NCU that was asked to preside over Mr. Floyd's first memorial service, held in Minneapolis.

At the service and across multiple TV networks that reached around the world, President Hagan issued a challenge to every university president to fund at their college or university a George Floyd Memorial Scholarship that focuses on offering scholarships to African American young men. But President Hagan and NCU answered this challenge first by committing more than $50,000 to start their scholarship. More money followed but even more important, university and college presidents from across the nation responded by committing significant dollars to also answer the challenge.

Both of these pastors—Jeff and Scott—modeled the type of action-based leadership that moves beyond denomination, ethnicity, or partisan politics and into a Christocentric focus that is tangible, transparent, and intentional. I can't imagine being a member of a predominantly white church where leadership's response to events was deafening silence. It would be clear for me, at that moment, that I, as a Christian African American, would undoubtedly be in the wrong place. The choice for me would have been very easy—I've got to be in a church that not only preaches the Gospel but lives it.

My church, Stones Church, is predominantly people of color, and Pastor Joel Brooks had rarely addressed issues of race or racism.

This was a sensitive area for him as a person who was very active in the Black Power movement in the sixties. He says often that he stayed away from addressing racism squarely because it stirred up too many bad memories. Memories of him getting beat up by the police or his father being unjustly treated. Being stopped simply for being a black man.

But when George Floyd was murdered, things shifted inside of him. He had to deal with this gross injustice head-on. He felt compelled by the Spirit of God to say it clearly, candidly, and boldly: This was wrong, ungodly, demonic, and it was the responsibility of every Christian to get involved and active in coming together to fight evil and injustice, no matter the color. In the weeks after the killing of George Floyd, I am blessed to say that Pastor Brooks began teaching some of the most clear, direct, and powerful sermons I've ever heard on this topic, and I've heard many. He boldly stated that wrong is wrong and sin is sin.

And as I write this, we are in two pandemics, one is COVID-19, which has taken the lives of millions of family members, and the other, racial injustice that has also killed millions of family members but is now on display, thanks to smart phones with cameras and social media. And even in this, I found that I had to push many of my white brothers and sisters to say something, anything. I even had a few of them, whom I love dearly, ask me, "What is the black community going to do about it?' I simply responded, "What are *you* going to do about it?"

Aren't we a part of the same family, God's family? If we are not saying and *doing* something about the injustices we are witnessing then, my friend, we are complicit in the injustice and part of the problem. It is in matters of being sensitized to injustice that I notice a sort of chasm between white and black Christians in how justice and righteousness is viewed.

An ethnocentric white Christian will oftentimes try to make it a "black thing," a "those people" thing, or even a political thing. But it is none of those. It is very much a "kingdom thing," because

God's throne sits on a foundation of righteousness and justice (Psalm 89:14). This is a "we-children-of-God" thing. We belong to the family of God, and when one part of the family hurts, we all suffer. And while there were some white leaders who spoke out, many remained silent. That is what an ethnocentric Christoconscious Christian looks like. Yet, Jeff, Scott and Joel reveal we can be more.

## Disruptive Innovation

The idea of disruptive innovation has to do with how things change. The question must be asked, "Am I going to adapt to the changes or am I going to refuse and stay the course?" Big brands all over the world have embraced the idea of change. Look around and you will see it. Christians should be the leaders where change is concerned, but too often we're the last ones making the changes necessary when it comes to diversity. We cannot continue to hold on to our separatist views and ways if we intend to remain leaders. And we should be leading people to Christ.

As believers, we must take an active role in fighting injustice in the culture and in the church. Christocentrism is action-based. Silence allows wrong to grow. How are we members of the same family, yet allowing one segment of the family to be hurt?

White members in white churches undoubtedly love God, but the defaults of American culture have allowed the growth of scales over the spiritual eyes of many, blinding them to the effects of the defaults on their brothers and sisters from the black community—as well as how it also affects them as white Christians. Quiet church services and white church music are not even the big divisive issue anymore. What has been keeping the black church and white church separate is the much more insidious problem of the defaults we are now uncovering, acknowledging, and becoming determined to eradicate, thanks to our new dedication to Christocentricity. And now that we've opened up some really uncomfortable but necessary subjects, in the next chapters we will begin to identify how to become the family that Jesus desires.

## Closing the Fracture

1. To be sure we're clear, write out the difference between *acknowledgement* and *blame* when it comes to our discussion of white church default.
2. What are some areas of the white church that are considered right by default?
3. What specific steps can be taken by members of the white church community to override the defaults?
4. What specific responses can be shared by members of the black church community when they hear statements that reflect attitudes or beliefs based upon white cultural defaults?
5. What steps can white congregations take to be sure people of color will feel comfortable and welcome in their church services until their memberships become more diverse?
6. What steps can black congregations take to be sure white people will feel comfortable and welcome in their church services until their memberships become more diverse?
7. Name two disruptive innovations in the area of diversity you can suggest for your church.

## Glossary of Chapter Terms

**Historically Black College or University** (HBCU)—Defined in the Higher Education Act of 1965, as amended, as "any historically black college or university that was established prior to 1964, whose principal mission was, and is, the education of black Americans, and that is accredited by a nationally recognized accrediting agency or association determined by the Secretary [of Education] to be a reliable authority as to the quality of training offered or is, according to such an agency or association, making reasonable progress toward accreditation."[7] HBCUs are open to all students, regardless of race. The purpose of the first HBCUs, founded in Pennsylvania and Ohio before the Civil War, was to provide "black youths—who were largely prevented, due to racial discrimination, from attending established colleges and universities—with a basic education and training to become teachers or tradesmen."[8]

**Harlem Renaissance**—A period from about the 1910s through the mid-1930s "considered a golden age in African American culture, manifesting in literature, music, stage performance and art."[9] The artistic and social explosion resulted from the development of New York's Harlem neighborhood into a "black cultural mecca."[10]

**Bigotry**—Obstinance or intolerance shown by someone "devoted to his or her own opinions and prejudices[,] *especially*: one who regards or treats the members of a group (such as a racial or ethnic group) with hatred and intolerance."[11]

**Disruptive Innovation**—Shakes up the market, dislodging the established competitors by transforming "expensive or highly sophisticated products or services—previously accessible to a high-end or more-skilled segment of consumers—to those that are more affordable and accessible to a broader population."[12]

# Build a Bridge to Unity

In my travels, I have discovered that three primary things bring people together: visual arts, music, and food. It's also true that we gravitate toward people who are part of our "tribe"—people who look like us, act like us, and think like us—people with whom we are comfortable because we have things in common. When we look around and see the more than eight billion people in the world, we must realize that we have much more in common than we have differences. Building bridges starts there, with the commonalities.

Bridges don't happen by accident; someone has to build them. And when we speak of a bridge having integrity, we are referring to the bridge being able to bear the amount of weight that will be crossing it. In our discussion at hand, the bridges we are building are meant to hold the weight of our relationships, and the integrity of the bridges is found in the trustworthiness of our words and actions. The relationships will grow and become strong based upon the reliability of our words backed up by the reality of our actions.

The experience of the Native Americans with the settlers from across the seas was not a positive bridge-building experience, to say the least. The settlers said one thing and then did another. Before they knew it, the original inhabitants were beaten off their land and confined to a devastating lifestyle from which they have never completely recovered. The bridges the settlers seemed to be building were but toothpick structures the Native Americans learned not to try to walk over because the bridges of fake friendship and false promises were proven to break under their weight and plunge them into pits of poverty, exclusion, and loss. After such experiences, one may just give up on trusting and look with suspicion on any member of the offending group. I'll give you a modern-day example. A couple I know are an interesting study when it comes to the ideas of diversity, inclusion, and innovation. They are both African American but have had very different exposures to white Americans, so their outlooks on race relations are very different. We'll call him *Jackson* and her *Annette*.

Annette was born in California in the late 1950s. Growing up, she never experienced being shooed away from a water fountain, being stopped from attending a particular school, or being forced to sit in the back of a bus. She grew up traveling throughout the United States with her family to attend ethnically mixed religious conferences where she watched as her father was one of the leaders in the national organization, seated right beside white men, and with the same level of authority and power.

Jackson was born in the Midwest in the early 1940s. He was a teenager and young adult during the American civil rights movement, so he lived in the thick of the madness. His father did not allow him to attend any of the marches and protests because Jackson's refusal to subdue his sense of personal pride probably would have gotten him killed.

Jackson's view of diversity and inclusion is obviously more cautious than Annette's. The Urban League was involved in getting him his job because white-owned companies refused to hire blacks; Annette secured every job for which she ever applied, whether black or white bosses were doing the hiring. Jackson and Annette's fourteen-year age difference, coupled with their disparate locations and the changes in the political climate, are evidence of how so many factors affect our relationship to and opinions of diversity, inclusion, and innovation.

But despite all of that, neither Jackson or Annette—nor any of us—is free to hold on to our personal thoughts about diversity, inclusion, and innovation unless they line up with God and God's words to us. This aligns with the Christocentric ethnoconscious life.

Revelation 7:9–10 (NIV) speaks to our mosaic:

> After this I looked, and there before me was a great multitude that no one could count, from every nation, tribe, people, and language, standing before the throne and before the Lamb. They were wearing white robes and were holding palm branches in their hands. And they cried out in a loud voice:
>
> "Salvation belongs to our God,
> who sits on the throne,
> and to the Lamb."

## Diversity: God's Idea

It's clear in these verses that diversity is God's idea. (Ironically, these verses have also been used by political pundits, social programs, and even churches to set one group at odds with another. But there's another powerful lesson in these two verses.) Notice that's since *every* tribe, nation, and tongue is represented—again, the word for *nation* in Greek is *ethnos*—every national origin, ethnicity, and language is also represented around the throne of

God. Diversity. And despite the diversity, the visible differences, all those worshiping are saying the same thing. Unity. How can this be? Diversity was, is, and forever will be God's heart.

The idea of wanting to be separate sets us at odds within ourselves because we were created by God to live in community—to be together. We've twisted diversity into social programs and political ideologies, but God has not twisted unity, which is His original intention. The Scripture is replete with the idea of different people getting along. What seems "weird" to you may simply be different to me. And therein lies the rub that so often turns ugly. We, as human beings, are great at trying to put each other in boxes, but people don't belong in boxes—boxes are for things. When God made you, He broke the mold, but He also broke the mold when He made your neighbor and the person you pass in the aisle of the supermarket. He made the person with whom you think you have absolutely nothing in common, and He even made the person you don't like. Yes, even him or her. He made the person who stands on the opposite side of your political ideology and your denominational tenets. (He even made the person who follows a different news broadcast than you watch. Yes, even them.)

> Just as our bodies have many parts and each part has a special function, so it is with Christ's body. We are many parts of one body, and we all belong to each other.
>
> Romans 12:4–5

> But our bodies have many parts, and God has put each part just where he wants it. How strange a body would be if it had only one part! Yes, there are many parts, but only one body. The eye can never say to the hand, "I don't need you." The head can't say to the feet, "I don't need you."
>
> 1 Corinthians 12:18–21

And yet, as Christians, we sometimes act as though salvation comes from those things—our political ideology, our denominational tenets, and our news channel—but salvation comes from one Person alone: Jesus Christ. And on this point, every member of the family of God has a mandate to do one thing: change.

The primary message of Jesus's earthly ministry was, "Repent for the kingdom of heaven is at hand" (Matthew 4:17 NIV). The Greek word translated "repent" here refers to more than remorse; it means "to change one's mind or purpose."[1] So, it would be easy to infer that Jesus was saying, "Change the way that you think for the kingdom is at hand." As I said, our number one quest as Christians should be to strive to think like Jesus thinks. This is about asking "What would Jesus do?" (WWJD) in reality and not simply as a trendy wristband.

We are spiritual beings having a human experience. In other words, we are spirit first. When a person gives his or her life to Christ, that person's spirit comes alive to God. At that moment, the one driving the car called "life" is Jesus, who helps us navigate by His Spirit to get us to the place He has created for us. The map for the trip has 66 books and 1,189 chapters—it's the Bible. And the Bible teaches that one's spiritual being—not one's classification in a "race," class, or denomination—matters most in all human relationships.

I will never ever judge whether or not a person is saved; that's God's job. My main question, from what I observe in society of some people who call themselves Christians, isn't whether or not they are saved, but whether they are healthy. In other words, does this group of people calling themselves Christians think like God thinks about unity? In one of the talks I give entitled "The Bearded Christian," my initial statement is that the unity of the church is a direct reflection of its maturity. Christians should be the most dialed-in, relational, mosaic-represented people on the planet. To be otherwise is to be so at our own peril and at the peril of our Christian witness.

Phrases like *white church* and *black church* indicate that we are not doing as well as we might think we are. It is clear in Scripture that Jesus is coming back for *one church*, and it will not be portioned off by color or denomination, although many of us act like it will be. Complete unity is actually a scriptural reality.

The joke is told of a man of "racial identity A" getting to heaven. The angel Gabriel took on the assignment of showing the new guy around. As they passed heaven's various locations, Gabriel pointed proudly at each amazing sight.

"There's the tree of life. That's the banquet hall where we'll enjoy the marriage supper of the Lamb. Over there is the entry you passed through from the pearly gates, and up that way is the royal throne room."

Suddenly, there was a loud, happy shout. The man looked in the direction of the shout in time to see a very large group of people of "racial identity B" joining in with the initial shouter. They were smiling, patting each other on the back, and hugging, all while praising God exuberantly.

"Racial identity A" guy couldn't hide the separatist smirk on his face, and Gabriel picked up on the man's disdain. After warning the man that he would have to drop his negative attitude, the archangel added, "I'm taking you to the debriefing area where there are more like you. Just like you, they thought they were going to be the only ones here."

How is it that extremist groups like the Ku Klux Klan and our post-Christian culture can integrate Christian principles into their rhetoric? How is it that Christian ideals have been taken and conformed to advance agendas that essentially have nothing at all to do with the unity that is in the heart and message of Christ? The answer: Religion is a belief system and sometimes systems get in the way. The reason the KKK and the divided church can be in the same room is because we must remember our nation was *not* founded as a *Christian* nation; it was founded as a *religious* nation. While Christianity was the faith practiced by the majority of the Founding Fathers, other religions and philosophies were as well, including deism. Once we let go of the idea that the United States is a Christian nation, what's happening in culture makes a lot more sense. The Bible is not the rule of law, the Constitution is.

In the next chapter, I will tell the complete story of a perplexing conversation I had with the president of a Christian college, a white man who could not wrap his mind around the idea that owning slaves was problematic. In this day and age, he still believed American slavery was something the Bible actually endorsed. This is how the KKK and the church can be discussed in the same breath, because unfortunately, the relationship between the two is sometimes closer than we'd like to admit.

## Dismissing Truth

Now, I realize that some things I just said are jarring and hard to hear. That's why we need new language that this book, the curriculum, the film series, and the entire "ecosystem" provides. I can be patient with my family members who don't get this. I understand. School has not taught us these truths. But just because the information is new, that does not give us the right to dismiss it. And once you know it's the truth, if you still calcify what you learned to believe before, you're saying, "God, I know more than you do." That's why I say I believe that the greatest threat to unity is idolatry. We must have the desire to know and to change.

## Today and the Future

As believers, our first allegiance must be to what God has to say about unity in the Bible. If we abided by the Word first, there would be no way to murder a man of another color skin and have church dinner under the tree where the body hangs. Unity in the body of Christ will be our calling card for a great move of God. When we name Jesus as Lord and Savior of our life, He is to be first place in our life. Nothing and no one else can have that position. One of the things I love about the Word of God is that it runs over everyone's toes. It calls all of us to change—it calls all of us to cross over to a deeper level of maturity. Sure, what you need to change may be different from what I need to change, but both of us still need to do so. It's time to mature more as we truly love the God who first loved us.

## The Way to Unify

I'll never forget an illustration I saw in one of our Sunday services that brought the idea of true identity home for me. He had five men stand up in front of the congregation: One represented a dad, one represented a man, one represented a husband, one represented a person of African descent, and one represented a Christian—a person in covenant with God. As Pastor Brooks went down the row of men representing facets of being a man, he made the comment that while each of these positions is important, the only one that, through our covenant with Christ, connects heaven to earth is the Christian or covenant man. This powerful illustration has always stayed with me.

Men can go to all the male conferences, fathers' conferences, and husbands' conferences they would like to attend, but if the programs don't feed them as Christian/covenant men, their entire being is not being fed. There is absolutely nothing wrong with any of those conferences—I attend them myself—but the part of my identity that connects heaven to earth is my covenant identity, and to be filled, I must come away with my covenant identity admonished, taught, encouraged, and strengthened. And Skot, a son of God whose heavenly Father owns the cattle on a thousand hills, can function at these conferences and in life side-by-side with other covenant men of any ethnicity. Period.

The Bible is clear: "So from now on we regard no one according to the flesh. Although we once regarded Christ in this way, we do so no longer" (2 Corinthians 5:16 BSB). In other words, every facet of our identity—every part, opinion, and ideology we espouse—must bow to the Lordship of Jesus Christ. This applies to all of who we are.

I love the chocolate-hued skin that God put me in. I love being African American, but I am a Christian first. My thoughts, ideas, ideals, and identity must reside in and come out of my relationship with Christ first. To put any other part of myself before my relationship with God and His lordship over my life is quite simply idolatry. An idol is anything that we have to get permission from first in order to obey the voice of God in our life. I believe that one of the most powerful and looming idols in society is, and has been, as articulated in the Old Testament reference below, that of the fear of man. The prophet Jeremiah speaks of an idol as a person, place, or thing in which one places their trust instead of trusting in God.

This, in essence, is fear of man. Jeremiah speaks to this:

> Thus says the Lord:
>
> "Cursed is the man who trusts in man
> And makes flesh his strength,
> Whose heart departs from the Lord.
> For he shall be like a shrub in the desert,
> And shall not see when good comes,
> But shall inhabit the parched places in the wilderness,
> In a salt land which is not inhabited.
>
> "Blessed is the man who trusts in the Lord,
> And whose hope is the Lord.
> For he shall be like a tree planted by the waters,
> Which spreads out its roots by the river,
> And will not fear when heat comes;
> But its leaf will be green,
> And will not be anxious in the year of drought,
> Nor will cease from yielding fruit."
>
> Jeremiah 17:5–8 NKJV

The first two of the Ten Commandments speak to idol worship. It is expressly forbidden to have anything before our eyes for us to follow other than God Himself. Exodus 20:2–5 (NKJV) says,

> I am the LORD your God, who brought you out of the land of Egypt, out of the house of bondage.
>
> You shall have no other gods before Me.
>
> You shall not make for yourself a carved image—any likeness of anything that is in heaven above, or that is in the earth beneath, or that is in the water under the earth; you shall not bow down to them nor serve them. For I, the LORD your God, am a jealous God.

The real root of this fascination with all things that "look, act, and think like me" is actually a manifestation of immaturity. Pushed to its extreme, it is idolatry. We should be getting closer to *childlikeness*, not living in childishness. Take into consideration America's history as it relates to slavery, Jim Crow, and other racially connected atrocities. To flip this, consider one of the greatest thinkers and scholars of all time, Frederick Douglass. He spoke about the distinction between the Christianity of the Bible and the Christianity of the land (US) and its justification of slavery to build the American economy from which we, as a nation, are still profiting:

> For, between the Christianity of this land, and the Christianity of Christ, I recognize the widest possible difference—so wide, that to receive the one as good, pure, and holy, is of necessity to reject the other as bad, corrupt, and wicked. To be the friend of the one, is of necessity to be the enemy of the other. I love the pure, peaceable, and impartial Christianity of Christ: I therefore hate the corrupt, slaveholding, women-whipping, cradle-plundering, partial and hypocritical Christianity of this land. Indeed I can see no reason, but the most deceitful one, for calling the religion of this

land Christianity. I look upon it as the climax of all misnomers, the boldest of all frauds, and the grossest of all libels.[2]

Mr. Douglass's words cite a prime example of idolatry, for how can you perpetrate unimaginable atrocities toward other human beings while reading the Bible to them and then heading to church on the Lord's Day? Why is Sunday at 11 a.m. still the most segregated hour of the week? This is a clear case of idolatry that stems from immaturity. Unifying the body of Christ will take more than event-centered activities such as reconciliation foot-washing services. Although such services are well meaning, it will take real heart work to fix our ethnically based problems. We can only get it done as we work together.

I saw a powerful film entitled *The Best of Enemies*. It's based on the true story of the unlikely relationship between outspoken civil rights activist Ann Atwater and a Ku Klux Klan leader, C. P. Ellis. The Klansman reluctantly co-chairs a community summit that is battling over the desegregation of schools in Durham, North Carolina, during the racially charged summer of 1971. The incredible events that unfolded would change Durham and the lives of Atwater and Ellis forever.

One scene portrays one of the best examples of idolatry in any film I've seen to date. The action begins with Ellis leading a membership meeting at their local lodge prior to going out and terrorizing a local white resident because of her having an African American boyfriend. Of course, in the film they called both her and him names. Just before they head out to do their dirt, they bow their heads and ask God to bless their work as they "serve" for the betterment of their "nation and race." "God bless us," they say, "as we terrorize, shoot, lynch, and burn in 'service' of You and the nation."[3] *That* is idolatry.

You see, religion and racism can go hand in hand, which is why I'm not quick to call myself *religious*. There's so much baggage attached to that term. Instead, I consider myself simply a follower of Jesus Christ.

If justice is so fundamental to the very nature of God, isn't it elementary to believe that it should be manifested in the life of every Christian, regardless of denomination, political party, or ethnicity? The only way we can dismiss what I would call a spiritual imperative is to ultimately put ourselves in opposition to God Himself.

## Closing the Fracture

1. What is a racial bridge-burning comment you've made or heard?
2. Have you ever attempted to build a bridge across the chasm of race? If not, why not? If so, what was the result? Does that bridge still stand?
3. What are some reasons people give for racial separatism? Answer each of these reasons with Scriptural truth about unity.
4. State the difference between a Christian nation and a religious nation.
5. Frederick Douglass wrote, "I love the pure, peaceable, and impartial Christianity of Christ." In light of our discussion about race, America, and the heart of Jesus, what does this sentence mean to you?

## Glossary of Chapter Terms

**Deism**—"A rationalistic movement of the 17th and 18th centuries whose adherents generally subscribed to a natural religion based on human reason and morality, on the belief in one God who after creating the world and the laws governing it refrained from interfering with the operation of those laws, and on the rejection of every kind of supernatural intervention in human affairs."[4] Further, "for Deists God was a benevolent, if distant, creator whose revelation was nature and human reason. Applying reason to nature taught most deists that God organized the world to promote human happiness and our greatest religious duty was to further that end by the practice of morality."[5]

6

# Overcome Disunity

Building bridges speaks to the extending of hands, the extending of the fellowship. This is the relational bridge. Overcoming hurdles speaks of the work that has to be done. Picture an athlete jumping over a hurdle. That person has trained and has put in hours and hours of work. Sometimes he doesn't want to put in all that effort, but the prize at the end of the work is worth it. Disappointment comes from unmet expectations, so it would be disingenuous of me to say there will be no work involved to change attitudes and habits in order to reach unity. Tension will be felt between letting go of the past, which is known, and grabbing hold of the present and future, which are unknown. To achieve unity, it may feel as though we're abandoning important things from our past, such as our brand of patriotism, denominationalism, or political affiliations, but what we're reaching toward is a much better brand of everything and anything we held on to before.

## America's Identity Crisis

Americans spend a lot of time looking back, but we only want to see what we judge as good. I think true patriotism involves loving one's country enough to tell the truth about it so as to continually make it better by correcting mistakes. And America's racial chasm is a big mistake. I believe God would pour out so much more of His Holy Spirit on America if we came to terms with the truth about our nation.

What we would all like to live in is a "more perfect union." Something that can become more perfect by definition is not perfect yet. We're a young country made up of imperfect people, so we have room to improve. To overcome disunity, there's work to be done to move us toward that perfection.

## The Hurdle of Sacrifice

This chapter is not about giving up history of our grandfathers' sacrifice in World War I. We do need, however, to give up that which has stunted the growth of unity. For example, many Americans want a narrative that looks backward and says, "Oh no, there were problems, but we've solved them. Slavery's over, the civil rights movement solved other issues; there you go, disunity has been handled. We've arrived." Then an incident like the murder of George Floyd takes place, and white culture dismisses it, believing what they've told themselves about the racial problem already being solved.

People are unable to face reality because we're not as good as we think we are. Everything is not okay. It's easy to lie to ourselves and dismiss a horror like George Floyd's public, daylight murder because we don't want to be associated with the shame it brings. We overcome this by working together. In fact, grab someone who is not like you and push against it together.

I remember spending time with a dear friend of mine, Pastor Ray McMillian, who along with being a pastor has also led a powerful ministry called Race to Unity (R2U). The focus of R2U is "the supremacy of Christ," with Race to Unity describing itself as "a ministry network of pastors and church leaders working collaboratively to bring about unity within the Body of Christ."[1] When I first heard Ray speak on the myth of a Christian nation and the supremacy of Christ, I took so many notes so fast that I think I made my keyboard start smoking. It was and is excellent information, but it is not for the faint of heart. It is meat and not "milk," in the apostle Paul's words: "For when for the time ye ought to be teachers, ye have need that one teach you again which be the first principles of the oracles of God; and are become such as have need of milk, and not of strong meat" (Hebrews 5:12 KJV).

The R2U conference is one I would love for every follower of Christ to attend. I had the privilege of transporting Ray to some of his talks. One of them was at a Christian college. I've heard Ray speak many times and I always learn something new, something deeper. His talks are transformational. On this occasion, I was seated in the audience next to the president of the college. The president.

The audience was thoroughly engaged, and Ray was doing his consistently amazing job at breaking down foundational myths about cultural Christianity. After the talk, Ray stayed at the front of the stage answering questions from students and others in the audience. At that time, the president leaned over to me and said, "Skot, Ray's talk was truly eye-opening. One of the best that I've heard." He continued, "I did, however, have one problem with it. Did he say that you could not be a Christian and own slaves?"

I looked at him, very puzzled, and responded, "That's exactly what he said. You can't be Christian and own slaves."

He looked back at me, puzzled. I couldn't believe what I was seeing and hearing.

He went on to say, "I disagree."

I said, "Are you kidding me? You disagree?!"

He then called over a faculty member to try to convince me of the error of my ways in a very scholarly and high-brow manner. Whatever. By this time, I was sure I was in a *Twilight Zone* episode.

"Skot, he said, "but the slave masters were nice to their slaves."

Yes, he said that. I responded, "Oh, you mean benevolent bondage. So, those slaves had a choice as to whether they could stay or go?"

They could see that I thought this was one of the most wrong and ignorant statements I had ever heard. I went on, "So you mean that you and your ancestors would have traded places with the slaves?"

At that point, I could see they realized they were in a debate with the wrong person. I got up, greeted Ray, and we headed out to my car. I must have looked stunned.

Ray asked, "What's wrong?"

I told him I couldn't believe what I had just heard, then I repeated the conversation I'd just had with the college president and the other faculty member.

He couldn't help but exclaim with both eyebrows raised, "What?!" But he quickly got over that statement as I sat behind the wheel, still in shock. "Skot, the thought that slavery wasn't all that bad is way more prevalent than you think. They were just bold enough to say it out loud."

Brothers and sisters, the aforementioned conversation is one of the best examples I've ever experienced personally of cultural Christianity—one of the most glaringly ethnocentric statements from those I would consider to be Christian leaders. This undercurrent of ethnocentricity as it relates to our country's past that is prevalent in the church is one of the reasons disunity continues and flourishes.

The president of a Christian college and a tenured professor held those views. How far off our theology can get when we stay in these safe circles where people think just like we think. In social science, this phenomenon is called "group think." Here's the actual definition: "Groupthink is a phenomenon that occurs when the desire for group consensus overrides people's common-sense desire to present alternatives, critique a position, or express an unpopular opinion" and the desire for group cohesion effectively drives out "good decision-making and problem solving."[2]

The US institution of slavery was one of the most demonic, inhumane, ungodly crimes against humanity the world has ever known. And sadly, many people who named themselves *Christian* participated in it. In fact, many of the people who participated in some of the worst kinds of terrorism were deacons and elders at their church on Sunday. The brutal bondage, humiliation, and degradation of fellow human beings simply because of the color of their skin was an atrocity that lasted for nearly 250 years—and perpetrators deemed this an acceptable practice.

Slave-owning was not simply sin as "missing the mark,"[3] but was a lifetime, a lifestyle, and an economic system built on the continual subjugation of a people, moving it into the wickedness and depravity of *iniquity*.[4] As 1 John 1:6–7 says, "So we are lying if we say we have fellowship with God but go on living in spiritual darkness; we are not practicing the truth." Furthermore,

> Anyone who continues to live in him will not sin. But anyone who keeps on sinning does not know him or understand who he is. Dear children, don't let anyone deceive you about this: When people do what is right, it shows that they are righteous, even as Christ is righteous. But when people keep on sinning, it shows that they belong to the devil, who has been sinning since the beginning. But the Son of God came to destroy the works of the devil. Those who have been born into God's family do not make a practice of sinning, because God's life is in them. So they can't keep on sinning, because they are children of God. So now we can tell who are children of God and who are children of the devil. Anyone who does not live righteously and does not love other believers does not belong to God.
>
> 1 John 3:6–10

Now, not every white person was involved in the peculiar institution of slavery. People like William Lloyd Garrison, John Brown, Benjamin Lay, and Jonathan Edwards all made known their disgust for and opposition to slavery. They were in the minority. Lay, a Quaker who saw slavery as a "notorious sin," addressed a 1737 publication to those "apostates pretending to lay claim to the pure and holy Christian religion."[5] Although some Quakers held slaves, no religious group was more outspoken against the practice from the seventeenth century until slavery's demise. Quaker petitions on behalf of the emancipation of African Americans flowed into colonial legislatures and later to the United States Congress.

## Hurdle of Fear

Fear attracts what we don't want; faith attracts what we do want. We cannot approach the hard conversations from a standpoint of fear or we'll never get anywhere. Living a life of fear is debilitating. We can be smart, safe, wise, and informed as we face the issues of this book head-on.

We may ask, "What if I extend my hands toward someone of another culture and they respond negatively or are mean to me?"

That's the risk we take, but we cannot let fear keep us from trying.

Fear is bondage; generational captivity has become normal, and a slave mentality has nothing to do with the color of our skin. Overcoming fear and captivity means we say, "I'm not going to let you control my life anymore. I'm reaching out to establish unity regardless of how you act or react." Fear of operating in unity is keeping us from so many things that are good; only Satan can be behind something like that. Think about it: What did the serpent's initial temptation destroy? Everything God had made that was good. Doesn't it make sense that he would continue to strive to destroy the good that God intends for us to enjoy?

God has created the standard of unity, and He's not taking it back nor is He lowering it. What are you going to say to God when He asks you, "What did you do about unity?"

A Christoconscious foundation without a Christocentric mindset is not a solid foundation nor is it a lasting one. Yes, I know there are many facets to our identity—age, gender, ethnicity, national origin, birth order, marital status, political ideology, denominational affiliation, and so on—but any of those incorrectly placed at the center of our lives leaves no room at the center for the God who made us. In other words, knowing about Christ and being led by Him are two different things.

This is how a white supremacist can self-identify as a *Christian*. This is why silence ensued while the lives of Sandra Bland, Trayvon Martin, Philando Castile, Patrick Lyoya, and George Floyd all ended abruptly and unjustly. It's why we as the multiethnic body of Christ showed no public display of unity during those injustices. There were too many pronouns flying around—"those" people, "their" neighborhoods. When pronouns such as these are used that way in the face of such ethnically driven atrocities, actions founded in ignorance are not far behind. Being a Christ-follower means to follow Jesus and not the cultural norms that continually try to shape us and lord themselves over us. I agree with Dr. Bill Winston who stated, "Justice is very important to God. In fact, it is the heart of God."[6]

By contrast, the covenant Christian is Christocentric/ethnoconscious. Operating through Christ as the center of life. These persons' thoughts and beliefs have been informed by the Holy Spirit and the Word of God; therefore, they are aware of their own ethnicity (ethnoconscious) but perceive themselves and other cultures the way Christ does.

To best illustrate what Christocentric behavior might look like, I'd like to add another example of when the church responded, in my opinion, in a very ethnocentric way, and then play out what that could have looked like if we were to have responded in a Christocentric way.

Let's look at another example: the death of Atatiana Jefferson in Fort Worth, Texas. A neighbor called the police to check on Atatiana's well-being when he saw her door open at 2:30 a.m. Inside, Atatiana was playing a video game with her eight-year-old nephew. An eyewitness said that instead of the police officer identifying himself at the front door, he went around "to the rear of her house, and in less than a minute, I heard gunshots."[7] In the dark with his flashlight shining, the officer noticed Atatiana through a screened window holding a gun. The officer demanded that she put her hands up and seconds later shot and killed her from outside her bedroom window.

If we, as the church, were truly rooted in a Christocentric ethnoconscious identity, there would, again, have been a lot fewer pronouns flying around: "those people," "their neighborhoods," and so on. The Christocentric response would have been for the church, the mosaic of God, a multiethnic, multigenerational, multidenominational body, to host its own series of news conferences and make an uncompromising statement about the unjust treatment and murder of Atatiana. The church would have then put together an action plan, and through its members who sit at all levels of influence in both this nation and the world, put serious pressure on the various systems that led to this case, and to similar instances of grave injustice that found the perpetrators involved not guilty.

The church—not the black church, not the white church, terms that have found their way into the family of God—would invest resources, human and financial, and show an unrelenting commitment to intercession to ensure that these types of ungodly occurrences cease to happen. That's just one example of what a Christocentric response would look like.

Instead, many from the church stood on the sidelines seemingly segregated and silent. Why? For many of them this was a "black" or "liberal" cause. Wrong. This was a kingdom cause. You see, in God's mind, we are the ones to administer justice, not only the Justice Department.

Isaiah 9:6–7 (NKJV, emphasis added) says:

> For unto us a child is born, unto us a son is given: and the *government* [rule and dominion] shall be upon his shoulder: and his name shall be called Wonderful, Counsellor, The mighty God, The everlasting Father, The Prince of Peace.
>
> Of the increase of his *government* [rule and dominion] and peace there shall be no end, upon the throne of David, and upon his kingdom, to order it, and to establish it with judgment and with justice from henceforth even forever. The zeal of the Lord of hosts will perform this.

Who is the head of the church? Jesus. Who is His body? We are, the church. Where are the shoulders located? On the head or on the body? The body. So it seems that the Lord has delegated and is expecting His body to be the chief administrators of justice in the earth. So, while we are waiting for Him, He is actually waiting on us. But oftentimes, we sit silent, cowardly, and segregated. And we, as God's church, are accountable for our lack of engagement. We are too busy *going* to church instead of *being* the church.

God helped me through a song. As I got in the car, my phone connected to my sound system and began to play a random song—*not*. Mind you, I have over 8,000 songs to choose from but the song that came on was from one of my favorite artists, Babbie Mason, and her song "I Will Be the One." The song asks the fundamental question of who the person will be who will watch, pray, and speak out for the cause of Christ. Who will answer God in the affirmative and say, "Yes, here I am Lord, send me"?

Wow. The lyrics to this song say it all. You can look them up and read them in their entirety. I love how they talk about unity, integrity, and being bold enough to take a stand in the name of Jesus. We must be bold enough to pray together, repent together, and ask God to hear our prayers and heal our land together. This is the Christocentric ethnoconscious life. Will you be the one?

Hebrews 12:2 (NKJV, emphasis added) says, "Looking unto Jesus, the author and finisher of *our* faith, who for the joy that was set before Him endured the cross, despising the shame, and has sat down at the right hand of the throne of God." The joy that was set before Christ was that we would be one—that we would live in unity with each other just like He lives in unity with the Father. If we have a problem with unity, and unity is something God enjoys, guess who has to change.

## Closing the Fracture

1. What is something you will have to abandon in order to embrace unity?
2. What is at least one fear you have when it comes to reaching out to start the conversation about unity?
3. Would you have said anything if you were with Skot when the college president suggested one could be Christian and hold slaves? Would that comment have agreed with or disagreed with the president? If you would have agreed, do you understand how you are on the wrong side of that issue?
4. Name an issue or situation in America that needs renovation in regard to unity.

## Glossary of Chapter Terms

**The Civil Rights Movement**—This was a "mass protest movement against racial segregation and discrimination in the southern United States that came to national prominence during the mid-1950s" and was rooted in the effort to secure federal protection of the basic civil rights granted with passage of the

Fourteenth and Fifteenth amendments to the US Constitution after the Civil War.[8] Using nonviolent protest, this movement of the '50s and '60s "broke the pattern of public facilities' being segregated by 'race' in the South and achieved the most important breakthrough in equal-rights legislation for African Americans since the Reconstruction period."[9] Victories came in 1964 and 1965 with passage of major civil rights legislation, but "by then militant Black activists had begun to see their struggle as a freedom or liberation movement not just seeking civil rights reforms but instead confronting the enduring economic, political, and cultural consequences of past racial oppression."[10]

**Cultural Identity Crisis**—The tension, discomfort, or distress that occurs "when our own cultural identity comes into conflict with what we encounter in the world around us or what we feel within ourselves to be true."[11]

# Avoid Cultural Ditches

I'm blessed to say I'm a Christian who is African American whom God absolutely, wonderfully, and lavishly loves. Some people may interject, "Why do you have to mention your ethnicity on there?" The answer: Because I'm both Christian *and* African American, and if you don't see that part of me—the African American part of me—you don't see a very important part of who I am. The only time I hear people laud blindness as a blessing is when they put the word *color* in front of it. Yes, I know what they mean, and their intent may even be good and genuine, but Jesus healed blindness. As I mentioned earlier in the book, color blindness is not a blessing; it's a dismissal of a critical part of one person's identity by another in the name of "Why can't we just be people? Let's just be human." We are. A beautiful mosaic from God's heart in all hues. Color is a blessing, not a burden. So, let's talk about what I call "the ditch."

You can't talk about ethnicity or race in the United States without considering historical context. Our sordid history as a nation as it pertains to classification by the color of one's skin has put us in a place where many people don't want to talk about it because it's painful. I understand where they're coming from, but I also believe that not talking about ethnicity doesn't make us any healthier. I mean, a couple of centuries of some of the most egregious examples of inhumanity is not a blip on our nation's historical screen. Slavery was not an "oops"; it was an iniquity. It was intentional. When speaking of the US institution of slavery, the abolitionist William Lloyd Garrison stated, "The compact which exists between the North and the South is 'a covenant with death and an agreement with hell.'"[1]

Slavery has created a callous heart in many people from all groups. I know that our nation's treatment of people of color—Native American, Latin, Asian—in general is wrong and ungodly on many levels, but for the purposes of illustration, I'll simply focus on the relationship between African Americans and European Americans, or as some would say, the relationship between "black folks and white folks." This relationship, specifically, is called the "peculiar institution."

Picture, if you will, a road. At the center of that road is Jesus; however, on either side of the road is a ditch. One side of the road is a ditch that is called white supremacy, white nationalism, and white superiority. Stay with me, it gets worse. On the other side of the road is a ditch that is called black subservience, black nationalism, and black inferiority. These may sound perfectly normal *if* your mind is not renewed as a Christian, by the Word of God, which says in Romans 12:2 (NIV), "Do not conform to the pattern of this world, but be transformed by the renewing of your mind. Then you will be able to test and approve what God's will is—his good, pleasing and perfect will." Both ditches are forms of idolatry. Remember, idolatry is anything you need permission from to obey God's will—any ditch being considered before doing what God told us to do. Notice that neither of these ditches are anywhere near where Christ is, on the road. Neither white superiority nor black inferiority lines up in any way, shape, or form with Scripture. The presuppositions of both sides are debilitating deceptions.

To my white brothers and sisters: As a white Christian, the notion of supremacy or superiority because of one's skin color is an idol. Now hear me clearly; I am not saying that being white or being of European descent is an idol. God made you that way, and your make-up is beautiful. You are just as much a part of God's mosaic as I am as an African American. But when one's ethnicity is used as a license to subjugate people, and as a license to reinforce that subjugation through imagery, language, indifference, and more, that is sin.

To my black brothers and sisters: As a Christian who God created black, the notion of subservience or inferiority because of one's skin color is an idol. Again, I am not saying that being black or being of African descent is an idol. But when one's ethnicity is used to limit yourself to the labels, narratives, and past that do not reflect what the Word of God says about you, and you fail to live out your identity and promise in Him, that is sin.

## Invisible Systems

When we hear a white man say, "I'm proud to be a white American," many of us associate him with a fascist portion of white America, and that's not fair. So we see that it's important to realize that we articulate ourselves in certain ways in an effort to acknowledge and celebrate difference. We have to be careful with how we say what we say so as not to be misunderstood. We have to speak with each other using the same definitions for the same phrases. Knowing what is heard is vitally important in order to be interpreted correctly.

God made us exactly who He wanted us to be. Believing in this doctrine of superiority (which is demonic) and the doctrine of inferiority (which is demonic) is the result of what has been tacked on over time. Even if an African American person chooses to believe that thoughts of inferiority were imposed upon him, it's up to him to receive it or not to receive it. This author refuses to sign for the package of "less than." Why? Because when I go into the Scriptures as a Christocentric ethnoconscious Christian, I can't see that I am at any disadvantage as a son of God—not at all. My rights to the covenant of God are not based upon my skin color, and God will never ever put my destiny into the hands of man.

What, then, should be done about the obvious inequities as our cultures try to unite, and who is responsible for doing something about them? Responsibility lies with whomever has the means to make things right. How exactly is this white superiority/black inferiority idea incorporated into the culture that is America?

We have to go back to the beginnings of what we call "American history." The foundations of the country were established upon the brutality and bondage of a people. The superiority/inferiority understanding is baked into the loaf; it's part of the bread. America had free labor for close to 250 years. In order to do that to a people, you must first have a conscience that has been "seared with a hot iron" (see 1 Timothy 4:2). That searing happened by creating legislation, laws, and a framework by which this subjugation became codified. Once the system was built, those building it backed up and disappeared into the walls—the walls we now call "the system." Now people just accept what is happening within the walls of the new nation and blame any problems associated with the system to the walls of it, when actually people were the architects of the whole system. The top people in office were almost all slaveholders, affirming the system and infusing it throughout the culture.

This brings us up to today. Why was the murder of George Floyd (to pick just one example) allowed? In the minds of the murderers—including anyone in power that day who could have stopped it—because George Floyd was not seen as being human, let alone made in the image of God. He was seen as a wild, dangerous animal who needed to be stopped at all costs. That idea can be tracked all the way back to the mentality of slaveholders believing that black people counted as only three-fifths of a human. That ideology didn't disappear, it just mutated from slavery to Jim Crow. White people, then, are no less liable for working against this mentality that remains in evidence.

This subjugation of black people is seen in the denial of healthcare; in matters of justice, education, and economic development; and in the structuring of neighborhoods, just to name a few eight balls that African Americans live behind on a daily basis. Systems built upon godless foundations are sure to fail. Here's just one example of a disparity as it relates to healthcare:

> Inequities in health create a tragic human burden in shortened lives and increased illness and disability. They also create an economic burden. Gaskin, LaVeist, and Richard, for the National Urban League Policy Institute, updated their research on the economic impact of differential health outcomes by race and ethnicity, finding that disparities in health cost the US an estimated $60 billion in excess medical costs and $22 billion in lost productivity in 2009. They projected that the burden would rise to $126 billion in 2020 and $363 billion by 2050 if these health disparities remain. An additional economic loss due to premature deaths was valued at $250 billion in 2009.[2]

Or how about a statistic that speaks to the possibilities if we removed disparities in terms of *spending power*:

> Greater racial equity supports businesses by creating a healthier, better educated, more diverse workforce, and by increasing the ability of minority populations to purchase goods and services. A U.S. Department of Commerce study estimated that if income inequalities were eliminated, minority purchasing power would increase from a baseline projection of $4.3 trillion in 2045 to $6.1 trillion (in 1998 dollars), reaching 70% of all US purchases.[3]

Perhaps you have heard of the term called *white privilege*, which we will look at more closely in chapter 8. When I would mention this term to my precious friend Rick Wilson, whom I called my Scottish-Irish-brother-from-another-mother and is now in heaven, he would freak out. "Privilege!" he would say. "Skot, there is no such thing."

My initial thinking about *white privilege* was that it is what it says it is. However, as God began to shape my perspective to more closely align with a Christocentric one, *white privilege*, as clear as day to me, became something a lot more sinister and deceptive. Why? Anything that is born of the flesh is flesh. Things born of the flesh are born out of death. Romans 8:12–14 speaks to this reality:

> Therefore, dear brothers and sisters, you have no obligation to do what your sinful nature urges you to do. For if you live by its dictates, you will die. But if through the power of the Spirit you put to death the deeds of your sinful nature, you will live. For all who are led by the Spirit of God are children of God.

Only things born of the Spirit of God minister life. When one stands back and makes an honest assessment of the seed, root, branches, and leaves of this "privilege," it becomes glaringly clear that this is a tactic of the devil that keeps white brothers and sisters in bondage. Yes, bondage.

While white privilege may be many things, one thing it is not is *privilege*. So-called white privilege is nothing more than bondage set in motion by the previous generations; it is bondage that was the idea of the forefathers and passed onto the current generation. The key to escaping from this bondage lies in repentance. And only actions prove the reality of repentance: "Prove by the way you live that you have repented of your sins and turned to God. Don't just say to each other, 'We're safe, for we are descendants of Abraham.' That means nothing" (Matthew 3:8–9).

Notice that John connected those present to their ancestors. Gone is the excuse I've heard ad nauseam that says, "Skot, I've never owned a slave." Sorry, that comment does not disconnect one any more than those in Jesus's audience could be disconnected from their father Abraham. They shared in Abraham's legacy. We share in the legacy of our forefathers, whatever that legacy is.

So this talk of white privilege is a deception of deceptions because it gives the sense of freedom but leads a person into bondage. God does not want this, but its allure and demonic shininess—Satan appears as an angel of light (see 2 Corinthians 11:13–15)—has taken many captive and into a place where their actions plant seeds of despair in the lives of others, who are unaware of who they are, only to reap a harvest of dysfunction, pain, pride and ungodly independence for which there is a high, real and unflinching penalty.

Please understand that I don't mean this in a mean-spirited way—that is the furthest thing from my intention. I love you; you are part of my family, the family of God. But we have to quit tiptoeing around the truth in order to truly heal. And don't get me wrong, we *all* have work to do, albeit the work is different for each of us. You see, this Christocentric reorientation costs all of us, but that price, my dear friend, is worth paying if it allows us to more closely reflect God's true character.

> But now I am determined to bless Jerusalem and the people of Judah. So, don't be afraid. But this is what you must do: Tell the truth to each other. Render verdicts in your courts that are just and that lead to peace. Don't scheme against each other. Stop your love of telling lies that you swear are the truth. I hate all these things, says the Lord.
>
> Zechariah 8:15–17

Sadly, the system of racism, bigotry, and prejudice is real. We have centuries of history that supports this reality. However, none of those realities can be granted the power nor influence to determine the course of my life. God's Word is more powerful. God is the One, in partnership with my obedience and faith, who determines my success and the fulfillment of God's plans for my life. If I believe a person or group of people has more power over my life than the Lord does, then I need to stop praying to the Father in Jesus's name and pray in the name of Steve, Bob, Bill, or Chad instead. Not gonna happen. God is God, not man. This is where the concept of white privilege falls apart. If you are a child of the King, why would you want anything less than kingdom privilege? Why would you desire the harvest of centuries of such terrible seed? There's nothing more sinister than an enemy trying to convince you he's a friend. My brother, my sister, the notion of white privilege is not a friend. The notion of white privilege is a Trojan horse sent by the devil himself, the enemy of your soul, to deceive you that this darkness is actually light.

## Love Is Inconvenient

You cannot love people correctly without having some measure of understanding of how they have been wronged. And if you don't understand love, true love, from God's perspective, you don't understand God because He is love. When you see family members being treated unjustly and say nothing or do nothing, I question just how much of a family member you are. Again, if you cannot agree with the fundamental nature of God, which is love and being against injustice and indifference, I'm not sure we're in the same family.

## Ubuntu

Ubuntu is an African ideology that says, "I am because you are." A core tenet could be summed up this way: To the degree I acknowledge your humanity, I'm more human; but to the degree I dismiss, ignore, or marginalize your humanity, I'm less human. Notice that the burden is on the perceiver, not the perceived. If I can look down on another human being, I have an unhealthy view of myself. Looking down on another person speaks to the insecurity of the one looking, not on the one being looked at.

The solution is the same for white people and black people. Be responsible for your position. If you find yourself as a white person acting in a superior manner, check yourself. Realize those you're looking down upon are equal human beings. If you find yourself as a black person succumbing to the belief that you are inferior, check yourself. Realize you are not what people call you; you are what you answer to.

## Closing the Fracture

1. What have you learned about how the history of America as a country has shaped current race relations?
2. List some ideas regarding what you can do about racial inequities in the following areas:
   a. Healthcare
   b. Justice
   c. Education
   d. Economic development
   e. Neighborhood structuring (redlining, etc.)
3. What can you do to break the superiority/inferiority system?

## Glossary of Chapter Terms

**Three-Fifths Clause**—While not making any effort to ensure that slaves' interests would be represented in government, "article one, section two of the Constitution of the United States declared that any person who was not free would be counted as three-fifths of a free individual for the purposes of determining congressional representation," increasing the political power of slaveholding states.[4]

**Kingdom Privilege—**

> Let the praises of God be in their mouths,
> and a sharp sword in their hands—
> to execute vengeance on the nations
> and punishment on the peoples,
> to bind their kings with shackles
> and their leaders with iron chains,
> to execute the judgment written against them.
> This is the glorious privilege of his faithful ones.
>
> Praise the Lord!
>
> Psalm 149:6–9

Kingdom privilege is to praise God and exert His dominion on the earth as His faithful ones. Notice that this privilege makes the lives of God's people *better*, while penalizing the wicked (those who have perpetrated injustices and inflicted pain on the lives of the *just*). Notice that *only* those who have a covenant relationship with Him are considered privileged. No one else. Notice that the wicked are held in *bondage, not blessing*. There is *no* other population on the planet that has privilege except those who name Jesus as Lord—and who walk in His ways, not just talk about His ways.

# Defy "White Privilege"

We've waited so long to do a deep dive into so-called white privilege because it's such a trigger. This idea of privilege has become one of Satan's chief weapons to make both sides bristle and find it impossible to talk reasonably with each other.

## Exposing the Enemy

The enemy we are fighting against in the issues covered in this book (and in any issue that stands against the ways of God, for that matter) is Satan. Satan seeks to infiltrate our thinking and cause division. You would think by modern-day behaviors that black people and white people, especially in the family of God, are enemies or even different species, but that is false thinking. We owe it to people inside and outside the body of Christ to love them as God has shown in His own personality—for God so loved the world. Satan is going after our witness as the family of God so that people on the outside of the church looking in say, "You folks can't even get along. We're doing a better job at unity than you are."

## The Deception of White Privilege

While Rick Wilson, the friend I mentioned in chapter 7, was fully aware that the notion of the US as a meritocracy is a myth, he wasn't aware of this term *white privilege*. Over the time of our friendship and together hosting for more than eight years a radio show called *Radio in Black and White*, that term continued to show up and gain momentum. I remember first being exposed to it in a local Institute for Healing Racism in what was called "The Privilege Walk" based upon the work of Peggy McIntosh. In the exercise, white people and those considered "people of color" were all asked to line up side by side. Then the facilitator called out statements. If you could answer yes to the statement, you were allowed to take a step forward. The statements were sentences like these:

- I can if I wish arrange to be in the company of people of my race most of the time. . . .
- I can go shopping alone most of the time, pretty well assured that I will not be followed or harassed.
- I can turn on the television or open to the front page of the paper and see people of my race widely represented.
- When I am told about our national heritage or about "civilization," I am shown that people of my color made it what it is. . . .
- I can do well in a challenging situation without being called a credit to my race.[1]

You get the point. First, let me say it is a powerful exercise and the intent of it, I believe, comes from an authentic place intended to provide healing, understanding, and impact. And in some instances, the exercise does all three; however, each time I either participated in it or saw it administered, something didn't sit right in my gut. I kept thinking about it because the end of the exercise saw white people in the front of the room, other people of color made it to the middle of the room, and African Americans stood toward the back, having barely taken one step in answer to most of the statements made by the facilitator.

I then went to another institute that was faith-based where the privilege walk was done. It had the same outcome. White people at the front of the room, some of the people of color at the middle of room, and finally, African Americans taking almost no steps at all. There are always tears as a result of this exercise. For some reason, though, at the faith-based institute, I was more bothered than hurt. I thought, *As a Christian who believes that God's Word is the most powerful thing in the universe, I have to come to terms with one central question: Is the Word of God more powerful than white privilege? Than racism?* Either the Word of God is more powerful than any system of subjugation or it isn't. As 1 Kings 18:21 says, "Then Elijah stood in front of them and said, 'How much longer will you waver, hobbling between two opinions? If the LORD is God, follow him! But if Baal is God, then follow him!' But the people were completely silent."

The day I took that faith-based privilege walk I had to make a choice. I was either going to give in to the idea that racism and white privilege had power over me and had the ability to determine my destiny, or God was the One to whom I should look to fulfill it. Kingdom privilege must be allowed to replace white privilege or kingdom privilege isn't real. I, as an African American, was created to reign, not to live in subjugation under any other human. Romans 5:17 states, "For the sin of this one man, Adam, caused death to rule over many. But even greater is God's wonderful grace and his gift of righteousness, for all who receive it will live in triumph over sin and death through this one man, Jesus Christ."

Praise the Lord! As we saw in the last chapter's glossary, kingdom privilege is explained in Psalm 149:6–9:

> Let the praises of God be in their mouths,
> and a sharp sword in their hands—
> to execute vengeance on the nations
> and punishment on the peoples,
> to bind their kings with shackles
> and their leaders with iron chains,
> to execute the judgment written against them.
> This is the glorious privilege of his faithful ones.

God always wants the best for us, and I believe that a foundational component of that is to be healthy from the inside out. Third John 2 (NKJV) says, "Beloved, I pray that you may prosper in all things and be in health, just as your soul prospers." White privilege has been misnamed and destroys the inner health of so many in a variety of ways. Consider the following thoughts on the misnaming of this "privilege" within the context of the spiritual law of sowing and reaping found in Galatians 6:7–8 (NIV), which warns, "Do not be deceived: God cannot be mocked. A man reaps what he sows. The one who sows to please his sinful nature, from that nature will reap destruction; the one who sows to please the Spirit, from the Spirit will reap eternal life." We have to understand that our acts and behavior matter to God and have a "harvest" attached to them. I call it spiritual agriculture.

- You will never harvest apple trees by planting orange seeds.
- You will never harvest peace and harmony in your own life by planting strife and discord in the lives of others.
- You will never harvest heaven in your own life by planting hell in the lives of others.
- You will never harvest freedom in your own life by planting bondage in the life of another.

Let me first say that what people call "white privilege" is an inheritance that gives people of European descent certain *material* advantages at the cost of a direct compromise to the way of Jesus.

I believe that for white people, it is much less threatening when they perceive white privilege not as something they sought out and chose (something a "bad person" would do), but something they didn't know was inherited whether wanted or not—which is exactly why it is bondage. The Holy Spirit's way is to convince them of this truth through revelation or epiphany, but a willing and soft heart is required for this to happen.

Everything after this realization is in their hearts and God's hands. As Eric Johnson, my friend and brother in the Lord, says, "I think that on average, white people are ignorant, not racist. That said, when you educate an ignorant person and they continue to choose their ignorance, that is racist because they just moved from making an unconscious choice to a conscious one. If they keep it [the perceived privilege], that *is* a choice. Will they choose to stay comfortable or follow the way of Jesus?"

With that said, white privilege is not a cultural knapsack of free passes, but an invisible noose of self-deception. It is something that makes its possessors feel comfortable while it slowly constricts their cultural oxygen, making it impossible for them to think fairly and to make equitable decisions toward other people—especially people of color. White privilege even makes people think what they have is simply because of their hard work, intellect, or virtue, or because "we know best." The foundation on which white privilege is built is the notion that its possessors owe an answer to nobody. All of the above is the great deception of, and will prove to be the death of, white privilege. It is, in fact, not a privilege at all but is actually what I believe should be more accurately termed *white deception*.

To the white Christian community: Anything that teaches reliance on self instead of on God is sin. Relying on yourself and on the privilege you erroneously believe you were born with makes you an idol to yourself, and idolatry always leads to bondage and captivity. Operating in this manner teaches arrogance, hubris, and inordinate pride, and pride always comes before a fall. Pride, no matter where it is found, is like an invisible noose. It strangles, suffocates, and destroys, and it does so while giving the illusion of freedom. God does not want this kind of life for you.

There are only two sides to this coin. A harvest depends on the seeds planted and even more so on the soil in which it is planted. In this example of white privilege, just as in the parable of the sower that Jesus offered, the soil is representative of the heart (see Mark 4:1–20). Either one is planting seeds depending on the law of the Spirit of life in Christ Jesus, or one is planting seeds trusting in the law of sin and death. From what spiritual law was the notion of *whiteness* set up? This will tell us both the harvest that is and the harvest that awaits. If you truly understood the magnitude of the harvest and the spirit of death within it, why would you choose it? Why wouldn't you want to identify as Christian *first,* which has its roots in a different foundational spiritual law? The law of the Spirit of life in Christ Jesus.

## Don't Take the Bait

Because the idea of white privilege has become the default in the minds of many white people, they have been culturally conditioned to accept what they think they are entitled to. Because of the deception in place, white people are receiving "privileges" all the time, and it takes a lot of honesty, bravery, and humility to step back and say, "Oh, I'm getting this, and I didn't earn it." Like a fish on the end of a line, they have taken the bait and swallowed the hook. They have been hoodwinked—what they think is privilege is actually deception. And all this deception does is separate them from the entire family of God that just happens to include black people as well as all other people of color. Does this sound like God's heart, or the devil's destructive plan?

## Don't Get Left Behind

There are those who acknowledge white privilege but decide to stay in it, and then there are those who acknowledge it and make a decision to move from it. Those moving away from it are advancing toward God's truth and sowing toward a life-giving harvest in both their lives as well as those of future generations. But those staying in privilege feel they are already in truth, so they see no need to move toward anything different. The "stayers" don't realize their bondage and are sowing toward a different harvest—but make no mistake, it is a harvest of death and destruction. And you must realize you're bound before you'll see the need to break free of those bonds. The "movers" have had a change of heart and now are operating, in technological terms, from a new motherboard. Their default is different now. Their new default is Kingdom—the mosaic of God revealed in Scripture. The old way of thinking that the stayers are holding on to is based in fear because to create unity is to first create a level of conflict. Jesus said there would be a sword that would even divide families. Matthew 12:50 (NKJV) states, "For whoever does the will of My Father in heaven is My brother and sister and mother." If white people intend to be Christocentric ethnoconscious Christians, they will be missionaries of destroying the deception of white privilege in their own homes.

## Come with Me

The Christocentric mindset makes the necessary changes and then goes back to convince others of the necessity for change. First Timothy 5:1–2 encourages us to respectfully speak to others about our point of view. "Do not rebuke an older man, but exhort him as a father, younger men as brothers, older women as mothers, younger women as sisters with all purity" (NKJV). Help pull others out of the ditch. This is what we're doing here: helping to reset the default.

## Moving beyond White Privilege

How can we move beyond white privilege? I would say that this is what all of us who call ourselves Christians should do:

> What can we bring to the Lord?
> Should we bring him burnt offerings?
> Should we bow before God Most High
> with offerings of yearling calves?
> Should we offer him thousands of rams
> and ten thousand rivers of olive oil?
> Should we sacrifice our firstborn children
> To pay for our sins?
>
> No, O people, the Lord has told you what is good,
> *and this is what he requires of you:*
> *to do what is right, to love mercy,*
> *and to walk humbly with your God.*
>
> Micah 6:6–8, emphasis added

Again, you see: White privilege must now be unmasked and called by its true name: *white deception*. Anything that teaches reliance on a people group or system in order for certain things to happen in your life instead of depending on God and God's system is, in fact, an idol and always leads to bondage and captivity.

Hosea 9:1–3 (with bracketed explanations added) exposes what idolatry does to all who are involved in our present discussion, to both the white community and to all faith communities of color:

> O people of Israel,
> do not rejoice as other nations do.
> For you have been unfaithful to your God,
> hiring yourselves out like prostitutes, [Idolatry is a whorish spirit because it gives intimacy/inappropriate relationship to something/someone other than the one to whom you have pledged fidelity.]

worshiping other gods on every threshing floor.
[Idolatry removes you from the place of true worship: the presence of God.]
So now your harvests will be too small to feed you. [The harvest of idolatry sets in place the law of diminishing returns.]
There will be no grapes for making new wine. [Idolatry destroys future growth from which you could have eaten.]
You may no longer stay here in the Lord's land. [Idolatry displaces you and puts you into a place outside of God's will, into a foreign land. It scatters you and causes you to be removed from "home."]
Instead, you will return to Egypt, [Idolatry brings you back into a place of limit and reliance on the arm of the flesh.]
and in Assyria you will eat food [Idolatry takes you into a place of greater bondage.]
that is ceremonially unclean. [Idolatry defiles you.]

There are six aspects that characterize white deception: cultural blindness, arrogance and pride, ignorance, self-reliance, the deception of inferiority, and the deception of superiority.

## Cultural Blindness

One of the key negative attributes of what I call white deception is that it makes it very easy for one to be culturally blind, and this blindness causes us to miss many things and people. And, though I am specifically addressing this within the topic of ethnicity, cultural blindness is a reality for anyone who has lived a life in which their circle of friends, information sources, and sense/definition of community has been seen through a lens that creates in the individual the false belief that their upbringing makes them superior to people from whom they are different.

Again, we can all be susceptible; however, for purposes of my focus in writing this book, I am focusing on what ethnocentrism specifically does to our white brothers and sisters. The attitude is sold as a privilege, intentionally or not, and that is a problem because a privilege should not be debilitating either covertly or overtly.

You see, the monolithic study of world history explained through the blind eyes of privilege leaves everyone ill-equipped to operate successfully in the reality of a multiethnic society and marketplace—which is what both society and the marketplace are.

While there have been instances in which a person has taken some sort of tragedy or negative event and turned it into a platform of strength and encouragement for others, this is not always the case. I think specifically of some of the folks who are sight-impaired in some way: Stevie Wonder, Ray Charles, and Jose Feliciano, just to name a few. What gifts these men were and are to our world! Their artistic contributions continue to stand the test of time. Though sight-impaired or blind, they refused to allow that to limit their artistic expression.

But when I think of someone being "culturally blind," I don't think of that as a gift that helps our world become a better place. Cultural blindness makes the world worse because it is often based in willful ignorance. When one neither knows nor cares about the culture of others, one is not only ignorant but is also prone to damage, deface, and defame the unknown cultures mainly because of fear of the unknown.

## Arrogance and Pride

White deception is fueled by societal momentum based solely on societal bias and sin, not on merit. This momentum is what I believe should be looked at through Scripture. I believe by doing so, one can clearly determine that not all momentum is healthy momentum. Momentum gained at the expense of other people, who are also created in the image of God, is not a formula for long-term success and carries with it a harvest.

Again, I think it's important to not think of this as something intentional but more as something that has been inherited. Language is very important here because who would resist a privilege? Probably none of us. However, when one takes the time to dismantle this idea and to dig into the fruit of it, it's easy to see that this concept is not a friend but one of the most subtle, yet debilitating, of enemies. And again, the most dangerous type of enemy is the one that pretends to be a friend.

Most of us have some idea as to what the fruit of arrogance or pride looks like, but it is important for us to be reminded of how God views it. If arrogance or pride is a fruit of white privilege—and it is—and God calls pride a sin, how can white privilege be anything more than deception and sin? And for the record, I've never met any Christian whose heart is soft toward God who willfully sins.

Proverbs 8:12–13 (NKJV) says, "I, wisdom, dwell with prudence, And find out knowledge and discretion. The fear of the Lord is to hate evil; Pride and arrogance and the evil way And the perverse mouth I hate."

James 4:16–17 (NKJV): "But now you boast in your arrogance. All such boasting is evil. Therefore, to him who knows to do good and does not do it, to him it is sin."

There are many more Scripture verses and passages we can reference, but nowhere in the Bible are either arrogance or pride a privilege. White deception is a debilitating posture of the heart.

## Ignorance

When you don't know what you don't know, you are ignorant in the sense that you are lacking knowledge as to a particular subject or fact. For example, you could be highly intelligent when it comes to biblical information, but ignorant about electromagnetism. You don't even know what you don't know about electromagnetism.

So take a deep breath. Ignorance simply means having a blind spot, and by the way, I'm the first in line to say I have them, but knowing and accepting the fact that I have them is actually a strength, as it qualifies me for God's help. We all need help of some kind. Of course, your need may look different from mine, but we are both still in need. If we weren't, why would we need a Savior? Why ask Jesus to reign in our hearts?

Think about it this way: Our weakness gives God's strength a place to rest. I don't at all mind being counted in that number. So, when I say ignorant, it simply means that a person has blind spots. The fact that we all have them is part of the point. The more of God's family that brings together, the greater the experience, exposure, and perspectives that are present. In other words, there are things that you see that I can't and conversely things that I see that you can't, and that's why we are better together than apart—we minimize each other's blind spots *because* we are different, not because we are the same.

I have no biblical basis on which to try to make you be like me. One of me is enough. God made us different because our differences—our diversity—more accurately reflect the face of God. Arrogance rears its ugly head when one of us tries to make others conform to our definition or standard of how we define or determine how someone else should be instead of encouraging each other to be his or her best self in God. The body, that is, those who are believers in the birth, life, death, burial, and resurrection of the Lord Jesus Christ, were never created to live separately from each other.

## Self-Reliance

Self-reliance teaches independence from God. God is never trying to work His way *out* of our lives. He wants to be *more* involved, not *less*. Remember, when we receive Jesus, God comes to dwell *in* us. How's that for a display of God wanting to be close to us? So the notion of leaning on our own ability is not only ridiculous but it was never God's plan. We remember that acting independently from God is what got Adam and Eve into trouble. Prior to the Fall, they lived in absolutely perfect communion with God. This wasn't to be a temporary state of being—this was God's heart and original intent for them. It was only when the couple decided to act independently from God that everything fell apart. Genesis 3:4–7 (NKJV) relates the story:

> Then the serpent said to the woman, "You will not surely die. For God knows that in the day you eat of it your eyes will be opened, and you will be like God, knowing good and evil."
>
> So when the woman saw that the tree was good for food, that it was pleasant to the eyes, and a tree desirable to make one wise, she took of its fruit and ate. She also gave to her husband with her, and he ate. Then the eyes of both of them were opened, and they knew that they were naked; and they sewed fig leaves together and made themselves coverings.

If the fruit of privilege—acting independently of God and depending more on an earthly, natural standing—is illustrated in the Fall, how is that a privilege? Is acting independently from God a privilege? No. Acting independently from God develops a sense of self-determination that is both unhealthy and ungodly. Those of us who see ourselves as privileged or existing in a place that gives societal latitude or permissions to do certain things disqualify ourselves from the honor of walking in the fullness of our God-given purpose.

The other side of the coin is the fact that others not of the same ethnicity feel that they are not afforded the same options (or privilege) as those who seemingly have this advantage. One simple question: Why would you want to? The position of the privileged ones creates a false feeling of security, arrogance, and a strong sense of what was Adam and Eve's downfall: independence. The idea that one can function independent of God is the essence of original sin. We were never created to live independent of God; we were created to live dependent on God.

As Christians, we must look into the mirror and ask ourselves:

Am I a culture-centered Christian or a Christ-centered Christian?

## The Deception of Inferiority

The hole in the soul of many African Americans is the deception of inferiority. Thanks to the ongoing brainwashing techniques perpetrated on African Americans during slavery, through the Jim Crow era and beyond, many black people have been convinced that they are less. The truth is that we, as a community, are better than we think we are, but in order to see that we must make it an everyday practice to become students of our surpluses instead of our deficits, our strengths instead of our weaknesses, our beauty instead of our blemishes, and when studying our history, also study our past that preceded both the civil rights and the Middle Passage. We have to understand that there is so much more, so very much more, to us as a people who God Himself created and put in this earth, not to struggle, but to manifest, along with all of our other precious brothers and sisters, the awesome glory of God.

## The Deception of Superiority

A hole in the soul of the European American is the deception of superiority that causes members of this community to believe they are better than other ethnicities. And by the way, you may be saying, "But Skot, I don't feel superior, that's the furthest thing from my heart and mind." This may be absolutely true. Actually, this is not as much an individual feeling as it is something that is continually reinforced in culture. I must say that the deception of superiority is the energy cell at the core of all that white privilege purports to be. I have found what I believe to be a useful set of questions (see Closing the Fracture at the end of this chapter) for us to consider with the intent of helping us better understand that it is more of a societal framework than it is a person's individual choice.

Let's allow Dr. Martin Luther King Jr. to speak again and sum up our discussion on this matter. His words applied here are as poignant today as they were when first written in 1963:

> First, I must confess that over the past few years I have been gravely disappointed with the white moderate. I have almost reached the regrettable conclusion that the Negro's great stumbling block in the stride toward freedom is not the White Citizen's Counciler or the Ku Klux Klanner, but the white moderate who is more devoted to "order" than to justice; who prefers a negative peace which is the absence of tension to a positive peace which is the presence of justice; who constantly says, "I agree with you in the goal you seek, but I can't agree with your methods of direct action"; who paternalistically feels that he can set the timetable for another man's freedom; who lives by the myth of time and who constantly advises the Negro to wait until a "more convenient season." Shallow understanding from people of good will is more frustrating than absolute misunderstanding from people of ill will. Lukewarm acceptance is much more bewildering than outright rejection.[2]

## Closing the Fracture

1. Who is the real enemy and how is he causing the fracture between white and black people in the church?
2. How is white privilege actually a deception?
3. As a Christocentric white person, what can you do to start eliminating the deception of white privilege?

4. As a Christocentric black person, what can you do to start eliminating the deception of white privilege?
5. Why is it not true to say, "I don't see color"?

## Glossary of Chapter Terms

**Meritocracy**—"The notion of a political system in which economic goods and/or political power are vested in individual people based on talent, effort, and achievement, rather than wealth or social class. Advancement in such a system is based on performance, as measured through examination or demonstrated achievement."[3] Landing a job because one has higher qualifications would be an example of meritocratic action because in such a case "you'd get the job purely based on your ability to outdo your competitors and not based on factors like nepotism or politicking."[4]

# Abandon "Black Inferiority"

Now, before we get too excited about the tearing down of the deception and idol of white superiority, let's take a look at the deception of black inferiority. Black inferiority is an idol for the same reason the idea of white superiority is. Black inferiority has been allowed to become an idol because many African Americans feel as though they need to get permission from white culture before doing God's will. In other words, for many of us, the dictates of the idol of black inferiority come before the dictates of the Word of God. The first and second commandments expressly forbid idolatry, and 1 Kings 18:21 (NKJV) asks, "How long will you falter between two opinions? If the LORD is God, follow Him; but if Baal [in this case, white superiority], follow him." Additionally, for people of color, and for African Americans specifically, this is a destiny issue.

The idolatry of black inferiority causes some African Americans to miss God's destiny for their lives while waiting for permission from someone else or something else before doing what God has placed in their hearts. But the noise and yelling of society telling them what they can't have, what they can't do, where they can't go, and what they can't become is so loud that it distracts them into actually believing all that is being said about them as an African American. So instead of praying in the name of Jesus, they start praying in the name of the statistics. They are bowing down at the altar of societal statistics, wealth-gap disparities, reports, data, and corporate glass ceilings. On the contrary, they should be taking God at His Word, believing God's promises and revealed will to raise them up, honor them, love them, and prosper them. It's already in The Book.

## Acknowledge the Struggle, Reject the Label

I am not saying that a change of mindset will erase the continuing existence of racism, bigotry, discrimination, and prejudice, as there are many people who have given themselves over to such wickedness. I am saying that God's Word is more powerful than any of these, and it is the divine Word of God that gives African Americans the power to refuse to let any of these things keep us from fulfilling the destiny God has for us.

I believe that God is going to hold us as African Americans responsible for abrogating to white culture, whiteness, and white people our responsibility to fulfill our calling and destiny, instead of believing in, trusting in, and putting our faith in Him to fulfill our destiny and calling.

I actually think the call to fulfill our destiny is a matter of stewardship, as in the parable of the talents recorded in Matthew 25:14–30 in which servants were given differing amounts of money. One received five, another two, and the other one. The one given the five talents doubled the master's investment from five to ten. The one given two talents also doubled the master's investment, from two to four. Both of those servants were rewarded with more and complimented by their master. In stark contrast to the stewards who started with five and two, the steward who had been entrusted with one talent hid what he had been given and gained nothing. When the master heard of this servant's poor performance, he did not compliment him, but reprimanded him because he allowed fear of losing the one talent to prevent him from using what he had been given for the master's increase.

I feel as though we, as African Americans, have come to identify with the servant who hid what he had been given. We are an amazing, blessed culture of peoples, so much more than many of us think of ourselves. Civilization and the first man and woman came out of the continent of Africa, not Europe. The first university was not in Europe but in Fez, Morocco. That's Africa too. Sometimes I think we, as African Americans, are subject to cultural amnesia, forgetting where we came from. We come from greatness. Period.

Yet it seems that we have rehearsed struggle for so long that after generation upon generation of passing it on as a part of our narrative, that struggle has *become* our narrative. And we are so much more than our struggle.

## Don't Rehearse the Narrative of Struggle

The narrative of struggle almost seems ubiquitous. At times it feels like one is judged as being authentically part of the black culture only if one has a story of struggle. It feels like this is how one obtains or maintains what many African Americans sometimes call our "black card."

By the way, if struggle and upbringing verify authenticity, well, I know I am definitely authentic since I was born out of wedlock to an amazing single mom. We spent some time on federal assistance (welfare) while my mom got her first college degree. In fact, I learned my reading fundamentals tagging along with her to college classes. I was the official family photographer at her graduation. She went on to get her master's and lead a nationally recognized school that was located in the inner city of Grand Rapids, Michigan.

But African American people are so much more than the struggle. As did the Israelites, African Americans have seen God bring us through so much. For the Israelites, God's delivering them from Egyptian bondage, feeding them manna daily, giving them water from rocks, and protecting them from the heat and cold of the wilderness were all manifested miracles. What's interesting to me is after all that, they said, in essence, "God hates us." What?! Israel's response was a function of listening to the narrative of struggle forced upon them by their societal surroundings rather than focusing on the God who is above what Egypt tried to force upon them.

Then we want to start talking about the Civil Rights Act. Okay, that was really huge, but black people were not invented in 1964. We come from the oldest culture on the planet. So it's important as an African American community to understand our part in the global scheme of things. If a people, any people rehearse the narrative of struggle, internalize the messages of how broke down they are, those messages become a self-fulfilling prophecy. We must learn to move forward based upon the truth of what God's Word says about us. For example:

- You are the apple of God's eye. (See Zechariah 2:8.)
- You are above and not beneath. (See Deuteronomy 28:13.)

That's our Father God affirming that we were put on this earth to live victoriously. And as Christocentric African American Christians, we are obligated to go into God's Word and let the Word name us—not anything nor anyone else. We are so much more powerful and more beautiful than the history we have come to believe is our lot in life. African Americans are so much more than we allow ourselves to be. We cannot put our destiny in the hands of other men also created by God. This is idolatry, and we must stop bowing down at the altar of the myth of black inferiority.

Mental bondage is the residue of physical bondage. And the sensation of bondage has many of us African Americans acting and reacting as though slavery still exists. The Word of God is the only thing that will free African Americans from languishing in the deception of inferiority. We must stop carrying those burdens. We were not created to do so. In contrast, Christ's burden is light. His burdens don't weigh us down.

## Quit Asking for Permission

The analogy of a house and who goes in what door serves as an analogy for culture as a whole. Can we get to the place where all of God's mosaic stand up for all of God's mosaic to enter through the front door? This requires everyone to be perceptive and neither allow nor expect anyone to enter by the back door—and certainly not to have anyone decide to enter that way.

I'm exhorting my African American brothers and sisters to walk in who God made us—powerful, beautiful, wonderful, intelligent. There is no need to prove you're okay. We do not exist *for* approval; we come *from* approval. God says you're His child and you are complete in Him. No matter what is happening, God can create a way out. Quit asking for permission. No one can make you enter the back door. Go through the front door.

## Rehearse Your Destiny

Humility is submitting to what God says about you, yielding to the identity God has given you. Do not let anyone else name you; repeat what God says about you. Take upon yourself God's words and repeat that narrative for your life. My African American brothers and sisters, adopt God's narrative that says, "I love you. You're the apple of my eye. I've equipped you. You were put on this earth to reign as kings and priests." I'm going to take that narrative, and by doing that, I'm exercising humility because I'm saying what He says, submitting to His Word regardless of how I feel. "For we walk by faith, not by sight" (2 Corinthians 5:7 NKJV).

I could have, for all intents and purposes, been a statistic, but the difference that kept me out of the stats was how my family spoke about our particular struggle. We never spoke about it as being pitiful. We regularly spoke of ourselves as strong, unique, and blessed by God. I was expected by my family to do great things. I guess you could say that the mindset in our household was that it was okay to be in the struggle, but it was never okay to let the struggle get inside of you. Don't let it define you; let it lift you. As my mom would say, "It (your identity) is not what you are called but what you answer to."

Rehearse God's narrative. Then believing it and living in it becomes muscle memory. The enemy wants us to recite his death mantra, to repeat all the things that are debilitating and to see ourselves as the victim. But never forget, God's Word says Jesus has set us free. We must allow Scripture to name us.

In my family of origin, an expectation to do great things was the norm. My wife and I expect the same of our kids (who we consider the bee's knees and the cat's meow, by the way). As I said, if there were a pedigree for struggle, you could say I've got a strong one. I feel like Paul when he wanted to provide his authenticity to the Jews. Paul told them, "I was circumcised when I was eight days old. I am a pure-blooded citizen of Israel and a member of the tribe of Benjamin—a real Hebrew if there ever was one! I was a member of the Pharisees, who demand the strictest obedience to the Jewish law" (Philippians 3:5). Paul was making sure that his questioners knew he had what some circles call "street cred" (or authentic credibility).

Here's the deal: African Americans' struggles are real. Have you taken an honest look at the disparities in various categories?

If you don't look at it through a Christocentric lens, you will be discouraged, and rightfully so if you are a person of color and more specifically an African American. However—and this is a big however—if Christ is truly your all in all and your source, then the faith that you have in God and in God's Word must reign supreme over the things that try to come against you to discourage or block you. Yes, racism is real, but God is greater than racism. It is right to continue to speak up and expose wrong views; however, leave it up to God as to how He will have the perpetrators give an account about their racist views, attitudes, and actions—and they will give an account.

## Let the Victory Name You

Covenant Children of God, put your faith in God's Word and in His ability to bring you into the destiny God has for you. There is neither a devil in hell nor a person on the planet who can stop you from fulfilling the destiny and calling God has on your life. Nobody.

You may say, "But, Skot, you are not in reality. Have you taken a look at the world and the state of black America?"

I absolutely have. As a contributing citizen of black America, I look at it every day. However, the Word of God tells us, "Don't copy the behavior and customs of this world, but let God transform you into a new person by changing the way you think" (Romans 12:2). Do not let the struggle name you; identify with your emergence from the struggle. Introduce yourself as the one who emerged resilient. The verse continues, "Then you will learn to know God's will for you, which is good and pleasing and perfect." The Word of God further tells us:

> Cursed are those who put their trust in mere humans,
> who rely on human strength,
> and turn their hearts away from the Lord.
> They are like stunted shrubs in the desert,
> with no hope for the future.

They will live in the barren wilderness,
    in an uninhabited salty land.

But blessed are those who trust in the Lord
    and have made the LORD their hope and confidence.
They are like trees planted along a riverbank,
    with roots that reach deep into the water.
Such trees are not bothered by the heat
    or worried by long months of drought.
Their leaves stay green,
    and they never stop producing fruit.

The human heart is the most deceitful of all things,
    and desperately wicked.
    Who really knows how bad it is?
But I, the LORD, search all hearts
    and examine secret motives.
I give all people their due rewards,
    according to what their actions deserve.

Jeremiah 17:5–10

It is clear in this passage and in many others that putting your ultimate trust in people will empower you to fail. In other words, putting your complete faith in a human being, for good or bad (in this instance for bad), is a curse unto you.

But notice what it says will happen when you put your trust in the One who rightly deserves it, God. It says you will be empowered to prosper (or be blessed). As you come into a greater understanding of who God made you to be, what God has for you, and how much God loves you, you come into the revelation that you and God are a majority. You also realize that by saturating your mind, filling your mouth, and basing your existence and identity on struggle, you are setting yourself up to live life asking permission—not permission from God, but rather from man. And as you can see from the previous passage, depending on humans in this way leads to a place of failure, frustration, and idolatry because you put your opinion of human ability higher than that of God's ability, and the last time I checked, man didn't create God, but it was the other way around.

I know this is a hard pill to swallow, but there is no other way to develop a solid grounding in a Christocentric identity than to begin to see God as your only source, period. As you grasp God as your only source, lay down the identity of struggle. You were never meant to have picked it up in the first place. The Word of God is superior to any struggle you may have, and His plans for you are victorious, powerful, and exceedingly abundantly greater than you could ever ask or imagine (Ephesians 3:20).

In some ways, to study the Israelites and their captivity in Egypt gives one at least some understanding of what happens psychologically to a people when they have been captive for an incredibly long time. The shackles transfer from the hands and feet to the mind. Interestingly enough, there is an act on Capitol Hill called the 400 Years of African American History Commission Act, which begins to try to address or at least commemorate some of that history. It says,

> In August 1619, the first documented Africans arrived in the English colony of Virginia. The group, recorded upon arrival as "20 and odd Negros," was part of a larger group of West Africans enslaved by Portuguese slave traders. They were on their way to Vera Cruz aboard a Portuguese ship, when they were captured off the coast of Mexico by the White Lion, an English warship, flying a Dutch flag, and operating under Dutch letters of marque. The White Lion transported them to Virginia, where they were put ashore at Old Point Comfort, in what is now Hampton, Virginia, and sold as involuntary laborers or indentured servants. Slavery had not been institutionalized at that point so these Africans were informed they would work under contract for a certain period of time before being granted freedom and the rights afforded other settlers. White indentured servants were listed along with their year of expected freedom whereas no such year accompanied the names of the African indentured servants.

> The historic arrival of the group of "20 and odd Negros" marked the beginning of the trend in colonial America where people of Africa were taken unwillingly from their homeland, transplanted, and committed to lifelong slavery and racial discrimination.
>
> August 2019 marked 400 years since the first arrival of Africans to present day America. There is an interest in commemorating the contributions that Americans of African descent have made to help shape the cultural, academic, social, economic, and moral attributes of this nation. A federal "400 Years of African-American History Commission" would mark this historic heritage.[1]

African Americans are so much more beautiful, so much more powerful, and so much greater than having to remain trapped within the shackles of our own minds. The reach of mental chains seems to know no boundaries; they are not confined to those in particular professions or of certain socioeconomic status. From the esteemed and hallowed chairs of African American-owned barber shops to senior executives at Fortune 500 companies to some of the most highly esteemed comedians and entertainers to many African American Christians who shout about having the victory on Sundays, I've seen this shackled mindset all over the place. Its existence is not without a real and significant basis. In fact, there are 400 years of reasons why this mindset would be hard to escape.

Again, the journey of African Americans as it relates to captivity and generational oppression is in many ways similar to that of the Jews when they were captive in ancient Egypt. However, with all that being said, we must still decide from whom we are going to take our destiny cue and derive our identity. Is it from systems saturated in bias, racism, and bigotry, or do we take our cue from God's Word? I will remind you yet again of the words of the Prophet Elijah, "How long will you halt and limp between two opinions? If the Lord is God, follow Him! But if Baal, then follow him. And the people did not answer him a word" (1 Kings 18:21 AMPC).

I think one of the reasons the people didn't answer Elijah is because they actually had to think about it. This is clearly plausible, as the Scripture illustrates this by the lives they were living in which it was common for many of them to have their own gods. In our case, let Baal represent institutionalized racism, bigotry, bias, etc., and, well, let God represent God.

Again, please hear me clearly: I am not saying the struggle isn't real. What I am saying is that we, as African Americans must quit asking for permission from humans to fulfill our destiny. It is not in other people's hands. Fulfillment of our destiny is in God's hands, and in ours.

Do you see how the notions of both white superiority and black inferiority are at their core demonic deceptions and idols? And both groups—and everyone in between—will be held accountable to God for what they did with what they were given. God expects to get an abundant return on His investment in us—the life of God's Son and our Lord and Savior Jesus Christ.

Yes, God wants a return on His investment. Here's something to remember: "God does not judge us for who we are but for who we refuse to become."

Let no one stop you from *becoming*. Yes, people have done and continue to do evil things, but don't think that God doesn't see it and that there is no penalty. God's Word says, "Everyone who believes in him will never be ashamed" (Romans 10:11 ISV). While God absolutely loves our various ethnicities and some facets of our culture, He wants to be the only One we look to in defining who we are. The differences between a Christocentric ethnoconscious identity and an ethnocentric Christoconscious identity are legion; they are as far apart as the east is from the west.

## Closing the Fracture

1. Define black inferiority.
2. Why is black inferiority an idol?

3. As a black Christocentric Christian, what can you do to combat black inferiority?
4. As a white Christocentric Christian, what can you do to combat black inferiority?
5. Cite a phrase that would be uttered by someone who identifies with black inferiority. Without using the words *no* or *not*, what would be the opposite of this phrase proving that a new narrative has been adopted?

## Glossary of Chapter Terms

**The First University(ies)**—The **University of al-Qarawiyyin** (Karaouine, Quaraouiyine) in Fez, Morocco is recognized as the world's first university by UNESCO and Guinness World Records, among others. It was founded by a woman, Fatima al-Fihri, in 859 as a mosque-religious school/college, and the school "subsequently became one of the leading spiritual and educational centers of the historic Muslim world. It was incorporated into Morocco's modern state university system in 1963."[2]

Notably, the four oldest universities in the world are located in Africa, according to research by Erudera.[3] While the University of al-Qarawiyyin is recognized as the oldest, **Ez-Zitouna University** in Tunis, Tunisia, was founded more than a century earlier, as a madrasa in 737, but wasn't established as a university until 1956. **Al-Azhar University** in Cairo, Egypt, was established in 970, and the **University of Sankore** in Timbuktu, Mali, was founded as a mosque in 989.[4]

# Appreciate Our Mosaic, Part 1

## Some Realities of the Fractures

The beauty of a mosaic is that all the pieces are unique. God's mosaic is made up of every tribe, every nation, every tongue. Revelations 7:9 (NKJV) says this great multitude is "standing before the throne and before the Lamb." Understand that we were not created to be the same. God loves difference, and if He loves difference, our trying to be like someone else is antithetical to His character. But also, putting others down because they are not like you is also antithetical to God's character as well.

When we consider the mosaic through a redemptive lens, we recognize that the pieces are different, but that they are also broken. The pieces build a beautiful picture when you put them together, but apart from connection with the others, each is just a broken piece. We are each to bring our broken pieces to the Lord. Then the picture gets bigger and bigger, and God looks at it and says, "Yes, I can let my presence rest on this imperfection."

## Vulnerability Brings Us Together

We are afraid to show our vulnerability because of our brokenness, but when we're vulnerable in the presence of someone who loves us, and that person accepts us, we are even more endeared to that loved one. Paul says he glories in his weakness "that the power of Christ may rest upon me" (2 Corinthians 12:9 KJV). Glorying in our weakness together makes us more human to each other.

In the Bible story of Jacob and Esau, the brothers had been separated for many years. The last time they saw each other, Jacob had stolen Esau's birthright, so Jacob was scared of what Esau might do to him when they met. The night before they met, Jacob wrestled with an angel and got his hip knocked out of joint. And from then on, Jacob walked with a limp—a limp that proved he had been with God. When he met Esau, he discovered his fears were all for nothing because Esau was happy to see him.

Personally, I cannot trust anyone who walks (spiritually speaking) without a limp. A limp shows you are human and vulnerable. You are like me. You have faults. You get me, so I can get you. We need to show we have a limp (failures and imperfections) because it indicates that we've been with God, and that we shouldn't hide or run from one another.

## Forgiveness

We need to come to the place where, despite the discomfort, we can meet with each other—black, white, and every color in between—and just start to talk without letting conscience, fear, and guilt drive us away from each other. Unity is the place where we are able to experience one of the greatest manifestations of our inheritance as this is the place where God commands His blessing (see Psalm 133.) Instead of running from one another, we ought to stay put and learn to live together in community. When we run from each other instead of run toward each other, we are not a part of the solution—we contribute to the fracture.

## A Christocentric Identity Necessitates Forgiveness . . . and Sometimes Boundaries

There is no higher example of power than to have the power to punish someone for wrongs and not use it. Think about it, God certainly has both the power and justification to do so but instead He sent Jesus Christ to pay that penalty for us. He paid a debt that He did not owe so we could live a life that we didn't deserve. His example shows us that none of us has the right to walk in unforgiveness toward each other, although our shared history provides many examples of why many of us feel we have the right to do so. But God knows that unforgiveness is simply another form of bondage. Jesus came to set us free—truly free. Furthermore, unforgiveness prevents us from receiving forgiveness from the One who made us. Matthew 6:14–15 (NIV) says, "For if you forgive other people when they sin against you, your heavenly Father will also forgive you. But if you do not forgive others their sins, your Father will not forgive your sins."

A Christocentric identity necessitates forgiveness. This doesn't mean one is giving up one's ethnicity or assimilating, nor does it mean not studying or understanding the history that necessitates the forgiveness. Additionally, to point out negatives that need to be corrected does not negate the positive things that have happened. But it is important to understand that if behavioral corrections are not made by the perpetrator, and forgiveness has been expressed and extended, the one offended has the right to move away, not because they don't love the person who has hurt them, but because that person is hazardous to them; the person who has forgiven can move away with a clear conscience because they made the effort to truly forgive.

Telling a group of people, "Get over it," doesn't work. When you haven't thoroughly studied the history and walked in those people's experience, you don't even know what "it" is, so how can you tell that people group to get over it? That *get over it* phrase lacks compassion, empathy, and humanity, and often issues from the person who least understands. Would you want me to tell you to get over the things that have hurt you deeply? A person's history cannot be dismissed.

## Learn to Appreciate

The word "appreciate" has several levels of meaning. Here, we are talking about binding yourself with another person's story. One cannot appreciate another's story from afar—as when beholding a diamond, you must get close to fully appreciate its value and beauty. Dive down into the other person's history. When we get close, we can at least connect on the level of person to person. We understand smiles and tears, hurts, losses, and gains. The closer we get, the more we appreciate the uniqueness of each individual. Again, when we compare this to appreciating the beauty of so many other things that have had to endure the elements, we understand that those elements can also create beauty and uniqueness. That understanding should then make us realize yet another facet of the specialness of that person. In the words of Henry Wadsworth Longfellow: "If we could read the secret history of our enemies, we should find in each man's life sorrow and suffering enough to disarm all hostility."[1]

## Grace: A Long-Term Commitment

We must take the time to acknowledge our history, yet still move closer to each other. In order to move forward, we must acknowledge we've done something wrong; we have to be vulnerable, and give and accept criticism in love. Black people and white people have a unique history together in this country. Even though bittersweet, it's a history nonetheless, and it's worth repairing the fracture if our nation intends to remain strong and truly live up to its potential.

Jesus washed His disciples' feet after He had walked with them for three years. They all had history with each other. Jesus knew their story and He showed His connection with them by getting close and graciously serving them in this way. Then he told them to wash one another's feet. We have wasted years in this country trying our best to be separated from each other, rather than realizing we are all walking in the same dirt—and that we are made from the same dirt. Our connection to each other should make us close enough to want to extend the service of washing each other's feet. Our talk about reconciliation, like a foot-washing service as we conduct them, is out of sequence. Before we can reconcile, we first have to be conciliatory, to become friendly. Don't wash a person's feet if you have not (and refuse to) journey with them. In order to "re-friend" someone, you have to have been friends in the first place.

## Appreciation vs. Assimilation

Oftentimes, there is an impulse to associate appreciation of the mosaic with assimilation. The cool thing about getting to know one another is getting to know our differences. The celebration of differences makes a marriage and a friendship unique and fun, so it makes no sense to assimilate to become just like each other. An old USA metaphor was that of a melting pot. For example, people came to America and changed their names (O'Sullivan became Sullivan, Janssen became Johnson, etc.) in order to be "American." Obviously, nobody has melted, and that's an assimilationist model that didn't work. That melting-pot model has changed to a tossed salad, and then even further to a stir-fry in which our unique flavors are supposed to work together to make something delectable. In the family of God, we were created different on purpose, for His purpose.

## Don't Just Tolerate—Appreciate

I've heard many preachers say that we must be careful not to get so busy doing the things of God that we forget the God behind the things we are doing. The busyness of so much doing comes from a works mentality; but we are not human doings, we are human beings. We get so busy working for God that we begin to see people as an inconvenience.

One of the worst words I've come across in my work with diversity and inclusion is the word "tolerance." This is not the thing to teach because we tolerate things we don't like. I tolerate a hangnail and traffic. Toleration is a low, guttural, primitive disposition to have toward another human being. Tolerance lacks all the characteristics of God. Be honest, would you enjoy being tolerated?

## Welcoming vs. Belonging

It's not enough to make people feel welcome in your churches, your neighborhoods, and your businesses. Being welcoming is like being a non-racist, a seemingly neutral term that is so much more insidious than it indicates. We must lean in by being *anti*-racist and *pro*-belonging. One of the thieves on the cross beside Jesus asked to be remembered, and Jesus gave him instant belonging. There were no hoops to jump through; the man's pedigree was not questioned. All the man did was ask. What matters is that we all kneel to the King of Kings and the Lord of Lords together. We must eliminate our man-made requirements if we intend to complete this mosaic and honor God.

## The History We Must Know

The history we've created in the United States of America often omits inconvenient truths regarding our moral foundation. Why is this? It's because, historically, the people who had the mightier pen and platform at that time were the ones who wrote history. If we are truly to set out to become "a more perfect union," shouldn't we want to acknowledge and correct our mistakes to hasten growth? What does the absence of this national willpower tell us?

Understanding our history is not an effort to invalidate the good aspects of America, but rather to expose the bad. It's just like any relationship—we cannot repent if we don't acknowledge our transgressions. Additionally, healing is much more likely for those who have been violated when abuses are acknowledged instead of swept under the rug. Love, real love, takes vulnerability. "Loving" America, and even, dare I say, being patriotic, requires intense vulnerability. I don't know how you feel about this, but in my world, I often see people labeled as anti-American simply because they have criticisms of our country. In truth, I believe they love America. I do too, particularly as a result of having been blessed to have traveled around the world almost twice. But I also believe we have a lot of work to do. For me, giving and receiving well-intentioned criticism *is* an act of love. I only have feedback for things I care about.

Furthermore, as I provide additional framing of what America is and looks like, there is no "true" America, nor is God's mosaic complete without our Latin, Asian, and Native American brothers and sisters. Each of us, each tribe, plays a distinctly different role based on each group's history. During high school, I was honored to have been chosen to participate in a program called Up with People for more than a year. It was life changing. Up with People (UWP), still in existence, moved from its original headquarters in Tucson, Arizona, to its new home in Denver, Colorado. UWP is a global organization that, through its one-of-a- kind performances, spreads the message of peace, love for humanity, and respect for your neighbor through a high-octane song-and-dance show. But the show was just a part of the total experience.

Those of us in the cast had the privilege of doing community service by performing in homes for seniors, in prisons, in schools, and in facilities for the differently abled. In just over a year, by plane, bus, ship, and train, we traveled more than 35,000 miles and stayed in the homes of amazing host families all around the world. I stayed with a total of seventy-five to eighty host families.

While truly an amazing experience, it was one of the most intense things I've ever done. I wouldn't trade it for anything. In preparation for our world tour, we trained eight hours per day, five days a week in the gymnasium at the University of Arizona. To say it was hot, after running dance and exercise routines repeatedly, is more than an understatement.

I give you this backstory because one of our first shows was on a reservation in Arizona with a beautiful Native American tribe. After we finished our ninety-or-so-minute show, as honored guests we were given the significant opportunity to have them share some of their culture, stories, music, and dance with us. It was powerful to hear of the origins of this amazing community. Although just eighteen years old at the time, I remember two distinct emotions during this time of storytelling: one of cultural immersion and the other of anger.

I took in every dance, story, and song, and yet my heart ached as I heard of the early genocide by American troops during the days of the wild west. I hated seeing such a wonderful people contained on a reservation, as though the visible boundaries were there to reinforce invisible mental ones. I was raised to be sensitive to the plight and situations of other people. I was raised to never look at another person as "other" but as a brother or sister. Sometimes we may vehemently disagree with each other, but we are all still human beings created in the image of God. I was disturbed that day as we got on the bus heading back to the campus where our host families would pick us up, and I still carry that experience with me.

When we learn about the Native American/First American/ Indigenous American peoples, we find very honorable people who had already been citizens of the land they had inhabited and nurtured for generations. Let's be honest, the long held and complete myth of Columbus "discovering" America is like my discovering your car. That's theft, not discovery. This continent and the first Americans were already here long before Columbus sailed. The irony is that the new arrivals from Europe were escaping their own oppressive situation, yet they found it necessary to disrespect, subjugate, and oppress the people they found here. They were running from inhumane and cruel treatment that they understood was godless and without mercy; yet they thought it was absolutely fine to inflict inhumane, godless, and cruel treatment upon others.

The settlers broke covenant after covenant with the Native American tribes, even to the point of knowingly transmitting diseases that would ultimately kill many of them. I am not sure what type of twisting and perverting must go on in the heart of a person who would do that, and then lie to themselves, saying that their actions were the will of God. The Lord does not participate in this, or in any other kind of wickedness.

In the succinct yet extremely substantive "History of Racism and Immigration Time Line" in *Teaching for Diversity and Social Justice*, a series of broken promises and crimes of humanity against the Native American community are articulated. Here are just a few of the events that are still in play as relates to the dismantling of the Native American community:

**1790:** Naturalization Act of 1790 restricted citizenship to free whites.

**1819:** Civilization Fund Act of 1819 passed to assimilate Native Americans.

**1830:** Indian Removal Act legalized removal of Indians east of the Mississippi River to lands west of it.

**1831–1838:** "Indian tribes forcibly resettled to West in Trail of Tears. . . . Over 4,000 out of 15,000 of the Cherokee died."

**1835–1842:** Second Seminole War, as Seminoles resist removal.

**1845:** Texas annexed by US government.

Wait, it gets worse:

**1862:** Homestead Act allots 160 acres of Western land to "'anyone' who could pay $1.25 and cultivate it for five years. . . . Since the Homestead Act applied only to US citizens, Native Americans, blacks, and non-European immigrants were excluded."

**1868:** Treaty of Fort Laramie "agrees that Whites will not enter Black Hills without Indian permission," but the treaty terms are changed by Congress when gold is found there.

**1886:** The surrender of Apache warrior and leader Geronimo to the US army "marks the defeat of Southwest Indian nations."

**1887:** Dawes Act authorizes the breaking up of tribal lands, granting allotments to families, "leading to division of Indian territory and encroachment by Whites on Indian land."

**1890:** Wounded Knee massacre by the US Army "marks the end of 19th-century struggle of the Plain[s] Indians to keep their land free" of whites.[2]

All the aforementioned atrocities and broken covenants were done simultaneously as America was declaring itself to be a Christian nation.

It's interesting to me when people ask, "But what does that have to do with today?"

Obviously, any racially biased position cannot be justified because God's heart is clear in matters of injustice. He hates it, and there is a harvest for those who take part in it and/or benefit from it. As you look at this history of oppression, let's look at the current state of the Native American population. If one truly has intellectual and spiritual integrity, there is no way one can say that the past plays no part in the present. Below are just a few of the statistics (emphasis added) from an illustrative Bread for the World 2018 fact sheet, "Hunger and Poverty in the Indigenous Community."

- "90 percent of U.S. counties with the highest Indigenous populations . . . are also among those with the highest **food insecurity** rates."
- "The **median income** of Native American households is nearly $30,000 less than the median income of white households ($68,145)."
- "Indigenous people are twice as likely to be **unemployed** as the general U.S. population."
- "Almost one-third of all Indigenous people were **uninsured** as of 2013."
- "Indigenous women are 4.5 times **more likely to die** from causes related to pregnancy and childbirth than white women."[3]

As you can see by the disturbing facts concerning our indigenous brothers and sisters, there is much work to be done to learn more, to do more, and to rebuild a more compassionate and intelligent society, together.

In the next chapter we will explore more in the way of appreciating our mosaic before tackling the work of closing the fracture and presenting glossary terms for this section.

# Appreciate Our Mosaic, Part 2

## Further-Reaching Fractures

### At Home in Seoul

It's funny to watch the expressions on people's faces when I talk about spending two years of my childhood living in Tongduchŏn, Korea. What's more is that my stepdad and mom made that intentional decision to live in the village and not on the base. Talk about being culturally baptized as the only American kid in the entire village. So I had a decision to make: either to have no friends or to dive in and become a part of the local community. Of course, I chose the latter, and my life is all the better for it.

I've had the opportunity to do business in Seoul a couple of times. And when I'm there, I feel at home. I am so blessed to have been raised the way I was, to just love people without trying to change them to be like me in terms of culture and appearance. This sense of celebrating you for who God made you was emphasized to me as the right way time and time again by my family, and it is a gift.

Now, I completely understand that there are many wonderful Asian cultures with literally thousands of years of history, presence, and practice, but I've only experienced a few, having been to Indonesia, Japan, India, China, and Singapore. Sure, not bad, but there are so many more great people to meet and places to see in this almost innumerable cultural milieu. Going to the Far East is always such a rich experience. The buzz of the city life and the quiet of a serenity garden both speak to me. I've had the wonderful opportunity to attend church service in Shanghai, China, as well as an overnight prayer meeting in Seoul at Yoido Full Gospel Church, pastored at that time by Dr. Paul (David) Yonggi Cho.

The God we serve communicates through every language and culture on the planet, and nowhere is that more obvious to me than when attending a church service and experiencing the teaching of the Gospel in another language. And although during teaching you will be given headphones that allow you to hear the message translated into your language, sometimes it was fun to just take them off, especially during the musical portion of the service, to allow the Holy Spirit to minister to me through the language of a melody or congregational song.

I remember going into the prayer meeting at Yoido Full Gospel Church at 10 p.m. and not leaving until 4 a.m., and it feeling like an hour or two at most. I walked out so refreshed that although I had to report to the office at 8, I didn't even need to take a nap. I was supercharged and ready for work. Praying with your brothers and sisters in Christ in your language as they pray in theirs is an absolutely awesome experience. It's a foreshadowing of heaven. Every tribe, every nation, and every tongue. Wow, to be able to witness and participate in the manifestation of the beauty and power of God's global family—this is my prayer for every believer on the planet.

As you can see from this small glimpse into my connection to my Asian brothers and sisters, I don't consider myself an outsider, particularly as it relates to being a member of the family of God.

This is why my heart breaks when I consider parts of Asian history, particularly within the context of the journey of many in becoming US citizens.

According to Dictionary.com (emphasis added), *Manifest Destiny* is "the belief or doctrine, held chiefly in the middle and latter part of the nineteenth century, that it was the *destiny* of the US to expand its territory over the whole of North America and to extend and enhance its political, social, and economic influences."[1] I think of our Asian brothers and sisters and recall how some were interned in camps or forced to work the railroads even though they were United States citizens. People who held to the demonic philosophy of manifest destiny thought it not strange to do reprehensible things to our Asian brothers and sisters in the name of the Lord. Whose Lord? We certainly are not talking about the Jesus of the Bible.

No, the outcome of such a belief as manifest destiny is the work of a false conception of Jesus that can be known as *Plantation Jesus*—the personification of a system within the church that had Jim Crow as its counterpart. (See also the book I co-wrote with Rick Wilson, *Plantation Jesus: Race, Faith, and a New Way Forward*, Herald Press, 2018.) Nevertheless, the Asian American community stood strong, stayed, and exhibited a commitment to a nation that didn't exhibit a commitment to them. When we look at the Asian community, we see a beautiful people who are proud of their heritage and are contributing to the country and to the world on the highest levels. As I provided, with the help of the document from www.racialequitytools.org, a summary timeline for our Native American sisters and brothers, I'd like to provide some historical context for our Asian American family members as well:

**1850:** Foreign Miners Tax (California) requires miners who are not US citizens to pay a special tax. It was rewritten to exempt free white people, effectively limiting the tax to Chinese and Latin American gold miners.

**1870:** Naturalization Act of 1870 excludes Chinese and other Asian immigrants from naturalization.

**1871:** In Chinese massacre, "a white mob in Los Angeles attacks a Chinese community, killing nineteen and destroying the community."

**1882:** The Chinese Exclusion Act "prohibits Chinese immigration for ten years." Renewed in 1892, it is made permanent in 1902 and finally repealed in 1943.

**1910:** Angel Island, touted as the "Ellis Island of the West," opens, but it is mainly used "as a detention center to control the flow of Asian immigrants (primarily Chinese) into the US."

**1923:** "Japanese businessman Takao Ozawa petitions the Supreme Court for naturalization, arguing that his skin is as white as, if not whiter than, any so-called *Caucasian*. The court rules that Ozawa cannot be a citizen because he is not 'white' within the meaning of the statute. . . .

In *US v Bhagat Singh Thind*, the U.S. Supreme Court recognizes that Indians are 'scientifically' classified as Caucasians but concludes that they are not white in popular (white) understanding, thus reversing the logic used in the Ozawa case."[2]

## Spanish-Speaking Saints

To meet, fellowship, and even worship the Lord with people who are different is a gift from God. It's like God flexing power when you come into a space where there are people different from you and they share their food, music, art, or worship style with you. For me it is like breathing pure oxygen.

The Latin cultural fabric is vast and lovely—from Mexico City to Guadalajara to Sao Paulo, Brazil. I have a confession to make. I wish I had studied Spanish and Portuguese. I'm sure some of you are saying as you read this, "Skot, it's never too late." I agree.

Perhaps the day will come, but in the meantime, I'm still going to enjoy all the music and meet all the amazing people I can. And although I don't understand a word of it without some sort of lyric translation website, it is still some of the most beautiful music on the planet. No, this is not solely Christian music, but as I told you, I was raised in a family where music was ubiquitous and moving from genre to genre was part of my education. To me, the gift of a people is not assimilation but the manifestation of their cultural uniqueness, who God made them. Such is the case when I have spent time in the various Latin communities and cultures. When I think of this rich cultural tapestry, I think of the people, music, food, and art all at the same time.

Latino brothers and sisters are people who have been an integral part of the success of the United States of America. This is their nation too. I think of those who have served in the military, fought for their country as US citizens, and yet have had to endure injustices and hardships at the hands of many in a nation they have helped to build. Latinos defend and support the United States with levels of patriotism from which we could all learn.

At the writing of this book, our nation is in a place of casting the label *other* on many people of Latin descent, particularly those from Puerto Rico and Mexico. Puerto Rican Americans and Mexican Americans are Americans, not a separate designation. Casting them in some outside category is inhumane.

We are better than that. I believe that we can be better, but we must *do better*. But let's also look through the lens of lost opportunity. What if we actually got this right? What if we worked to close the gap? To me, this is far more compelling. I know these statistics may be way more than you'll ever want or need, but I wanted to share with you some other data that points to our need:

- **GDP:** "Minorities make up 37% of the working age population now, but they are projected to grow to 46% by 2030, and 55% by 2050. Closing the earnings gap by 2030 would increase GDP by 16%, and by 2050," GDP would increase by 20%.[3]

- **Education:** "A McKinsey & Company analysis of the educational achievement gap between African American, Hispanic, and white students found that closing the education gap would have increased US GDP by 2% to 4% in 2008, representing between $310 and $525 billion."[4]
- **Healthcare:** The National Urban League Policy Institute projected that the burden caused by differential health outcomes by race and ethnicity will cost the US "$363 billion by 2050 if these health disparities remain." [5]
- **Housing:** "In the second quarter of 2022, the homeownership rate for white households was 75 percent compared to 45 percent for Black households, 48 percent for Hispanic households, and 57 percent for non-Hispanic households of any other race. . . . The Black-white gap in homeownership rates was the same in 2020 as it was in 1970, just two years after the passage of the Fair Housing Act of 1968, which sought to end racial discrimination in the housing market. . . . Together, differences in the homeownership rates, home values, housing returns, and distressed home sales have contributed to large racial gaps in housing equity wealth that widen over the lifecycle."[6]
- **Spending Power:** A US Department of Commerce study estimated that if income inequalities were eliminated, minority purchasing power would increase from a baseline projection of $4.3 trillion in 2045 to $6.1 trillion . . . reaching 70% of all U. S. purchases.[7]

## What We're Missing

So what are we, the church as the family of God, supposed to do about this? While I believe there are many things we can do, one thing we must do is speak up as a covenant family—and speak up for each other. When we see each other through the eyes of the flesh instead of through the eyes of Christ with the mind of Christ, we will always miss the point. When not seeing with the eyes and mind of Christ, we will miss the opportunity to unify on a level that cannot be replicated by those outside the body of Christ. Sadly, in many instances, you can't tell the difference between those who belong to the family of God and those who don't. But don't get it twisted: God is bringing the distinction into view. Malachi 3:16–18 (NIV) states:

> Then those who feared the LORD talked with each other, and the Lord listened and heard. A scroll of remembrance was written in his presence concerning those who feared the LORD and honored his name.
>
> "On the day when I act," says the LORD Almighty, "they will be my treasured possession. I will spare them, just as a father has compassion and spares his son who serves him. And you will again see the distinction between the righteous and the wicked, between those who serve God and those who do not."

I am sure I'm not the only one who realizes this, but it seems that in the body of Christ, we are left sorely lacking in the area of the fear of the Lord. I've never seen so much hateful rhetoric, brutish bias, and lack of listening to one another as I have seen in the past few years "in the name of the Lord." If one were to just take the political environment as the indicator of the health of the church, one would think that our salvation came from either a donkey or an elephant, from the color blue or red. But the last time I checked, neither party nor color died for me to set me free; Jesus did that.

What our separation does reveal is our immaturity as a God-ordained family. Paul declares in 1 Corinthians 1:13 (NIV), "Is Christ divided? Was Paul crucified for you? Were you baptized in the name of Paul?" By the way we are acting, one could easily paraphrase this verse in the following way: "Is Christ divided? Were the [your political party] crucified for you? Were you baptized in the name of the [your political party]?"

Family, it's time for us to grow up or we risk missing the blessing of God that only comes through unity. Psalm 133 makes clear the importance of unity in God's scheme of things:

> How good and pleasant it is
>   when God's people live together in unity!
>
> It is like precious oil poured on the head,
>   running down on the beard,
> running down on Aaron's beard,
>   down on the collar of his robe.
> It is as if the dew of Hermon
>   were falling on Mount Zion.
> For there the Lord bestows his blessing,
>   even life forevermore.
>
> Psalm 133:1–3 NIV

Here's a note for all of us who are members of the family of God. Jesus said, "Repent for the kingdom of heaven is at hand" (Matthew 4:17 NKJV). Repent simply means to change the way we think. If we have truly repented, then we will act differently, because how we think and how we behave are inextricably linked with each other. So if we say we have repented, then our actions must line up with our confessions, and our new, changed actions should be visible to those around us. If our actions haven't changed, it's because we haven't repented. Period. And we find ourselves back at the altar of ethnic worship that held us in blinding bondage in the first place. It is only when we truly accept the identity for which Jesus died and rose to give us that we truly are made free. We cannot have a change of heart without God's help, and we all need a change of heart.

So why is change even necessary? Although one could write pages and pages to answer this, and many have, there is a short answer. We must change because God said so. God is right. Always. And because He is right, when we are wrong, guess who needs to change? We act as though God's mandate to love each other is an option. It's not. Self-deception is the worst kind of deception because it dupes us into thinking that we are doing something we are not doing at all. Again, we must be careful not to get so busy doing the things of God that we forget the God behind the things we're doing. Matthew 7:21–23 says,

> Not everyone who calls out to me, "Lord! Lord!" will enter the Kingdom of Heaven. Only those who actually do the will of my Father in heaven will enter. On judgment day many will say to me, "Lord! Lord! We prophesied in your name and cast out demons in your name and performed many miracles in your name." But I will reply, "I never knew you. Get away from me, you who break God's laws."

From the beginning, this country set out under the pretense of becoming a "more perfect union." Loving America is loving that idea. Patriotism is that idea. Love challenges us because it believes we can become better. Are we challenging the exposure of our history because we perceive it as a threat? I would argue that this is because we don't understand the power of vulnerability as a gateway to love—to true "patriotism" in the proud-but-inclusive sense. Love means having hard conversations, humbling yourself, and acknowledging your failures in service of a stronger, more inclusive bond . . . or in US terms, a more perfect union. And in the book of Micah, God defines love, obedience, and sacrifice:

> What can we bring to the Lord?
>     Should we bring him burnt offerings?
> Should we bow before God Most High
>     with offerings of yearling calves?
> Should we offer him thousands of rams
>     and ten thousand rivers of olive oil?

Should we sacrifice our firstborn children
to pay for our sins?

No, O people, the Lord has told you what is good,
and this is what he requires of you:
to do what is right, to love mercy,
and to walk humbly with your God.

Micah 6:6–8

## Closing the Fracture

1. How are people of different races/ethnicities like a mosaic?
    a. How does brokenness make us alike?
2. Why does forgiveness sometimes necessitate boundaries?
3 What does it mean to *appreciate* someone from another culture?
    a. Why is appreciation preferable to assimilation?
    b. In what ways do you expect people of another race to assimilate?
4. What is negative about the practice of tolerance when it comes to our relationship with those who are different from us in some way?
5. How have you been affected by your exposure to the points of history presented in this chapter?
    a. What action steps are you willing to take in response to the history you read in this chapter?

## Chapter Glossary of Terms

**Manifest Destiny**—Coined in 1845, this phrase conveyed the idea that the United States was "destined—by God, its advocates believed—to expand its dominion and spread democracy and capitalism across the entire North American continent. The philosophy drove 19th-century U. S. territorial expansion and was used to justify the forced removal of Native Americans and other groups from their homes. The rapid expansion of the United States intensified the issue of slavery as new states were added to the Union, leading to the outbreak of the Civil War."[8]

**Patriotism**—"The feeling of love, devotion, and sense of attachment to one's country. This attachment can be a combination of many different feelings, language relating to one's own homeland, including ethnic, cultural, political, or historical aspects. It encompasses a set of concepts closely related to nationalism, mostly civic nationalism and sometimes cultural nationalism."[9]

# Understand the Change Sequence

> But now I am determined to bless Jerusalem and the people of Judah. So don't be afraid. But this is what you must do: Tell the truth to each other. Render verdicts in your courts that are just and that lead to peace. Don't scheme against each other. Stop your love of telling lies that you swear are the truth. I hate all these things, says the Lord.
>
> Zechariah 8:15–17

The change sequence is simply the steps or protocol we need to go through to effect change in the area of reconciliation. The change sequence brings order to what we have been talking about and walking through in this entire book. If you have stuck with me this far, we've made it to the top of the mountain of this issue, and this opportunity, together. So now it's time to exercise what we have learned.

## Truth Is the Foundation

"But speaking the truth in love, may [we] grow up into him in all things, which is the head, even Christ" (Ephesians 4:15 KJV).

If we truly have a heart to change, if we truly love God, we must start by telling the truth to each other. What we have to say doesn't have to be nor should it be mean-spirited, but it must be honest. We've become so politically correct that much of the time uncomfortable conversations are avoided for the sake of keeping the peace, when silence is not what real peace is. Real peace is calmness in the presence of conflict.

Within the context of *Unfractured*, our primary focus is how a person moves successfully from being an ethnocentric Christoconscious Christian to being a Christocentric ethnoconscious Christian. This is a process I've termed the *change sequence*, and in this sequence, busyness is the enemy. I have the honor of working with many great organizations all around the globe. Leaders doing terrific work and making a difference team with me and my organization to reach further and grow stronger.

Busyness is often an excuse for not addressing the hard stuff head on. This journey from ethnocentricity to Christocentricity is a process that must be led by the Holy Spirit because it is impossible for a person to do without His help. Heart work is hard work.

But if we truly want a richer, fuller, and deeper experience with God, we are going to have to ask Jesus to be at the center of our life and to help us see all the other facets of our identity through His eyes and His eyes only. We must ask Him to help us recognize what we have failed to see as it relates to ourselves, others, and Him. This is where the first step in the change sequence begins.

## The Change Sequence, Step One: Recognize

We cannot reconcile unless we recognize. To *re-cognize* is to know again. I find that many people simply don't want to take the time to dig into history as it relates to the injustices and the early intentional structuring of systems that greatly influence our lives today. Many people don't connect the past with the present. To me, the more one digs into the past, particularly of this nation, the more sense today makes. While I understand that looking back can be painful, it is necessary. When some of my brothers and sisters tell me to "get over it," the first thing I want them to do is to define what "it" is. And in order for them to do that honestly, they are going to have to study history, not just their mother's or grandfather's version of history, but to go after the facts in an unbiased fashion. To find the truth even if that which is uncovered is uncomfortable. We've looked at some of the truths in previous chapters.

Jesus knew we would walk into some uncomfortable situations so He sent the Helper, the Comforter, the Holy Spirit who would "guide [us] into all truth" (John 14:16–17 and 16:13 NKJV). If life were about comfort, we wouldn't need this Jesus-supplied Comforter. But we do need Him.

One must ask himself or herself, *What am I afraid of? What have I got to lose if I surrender my racism or bias? What will happen if I give up the way I have practiced thinking all my life?* Actually, one of the very real answers is that you give up a false identity, the one built on an ethnocentric idol, to live in the non-idolatrous identity for which God created you. The idol neither saves nor delivers, but instead holds its subject in unrelenting bondage, the bondage of fear of what you might find out, bondage of the deception of privilege, bondage to the deception that you are powerless to do anything about moving away from this captivity that came with a misrepresentation of history. The worst type of captivity is one in which a person thinks they are free while residing in total bondage. Only Jesus can make us free. "Therefore if the Son makes you free, you shall be free indeed" (John 8:36 NKJV). Any belief system that leads us to a place of self-reliance where we derive the most significant part of our identity from our ethnicity instead of finding the most significant part of our identity in Christ alone will only lead us into a place of bondage, idolatry, and deception. Frankly, this is the place where many Christians reside today. This is why recognition is the first step for any Christian to begin their journey to true Christocentric wholeness. As the words from Edward Mote's beautiful hymn "My Hope is Built on Nothing Less" tell us, "all other ground is sinking sand." Our chief identity can only be found in Christ.

### Take the First Step

Take the first step. The more you recognize, the more you may become uncomfortable. This first step is the hardest and therein lies the fear. It requires bravery to choose Christocentrism over ethnocentrism. Because you are rooted in Christ, faith kicks in.

### Diversify Your Counsel

What messages are you absorbing? Listen to the still small voice that tells you when you are in the right place. Do not walk in the council of the ungodly (see Psalm 1). Do you know God's voice? You can know Scripture but not know God's voice. What does Scripture say? Isolate yourself from those feeding you the old divisive messages. Open up and listen to those who are different but who share the same precious faith.

### Leadership Matters

Hearts can be open but there needs to be leadership from both sides to initiate the conversations and get things started. Many times, the people in the congregations are much further ahead than the people in the pulpit. The pastor can't know everything. Someone once said, "Here are my followers, let me catch up to them." Still, it is the job of the pulpit to equip the pew, and if that leader is not growing in the area of his or her own personal journey as someone who is becoming more fluent in the biblical language of Christocentrism/ethnoconsciousness, the people in the pew aren't growing either. The leader who was silent from the pulpit the day after the George Floyd incident will have a congregation that is quiet as well. Like priest, like people. But these people are going from church back into their companies and neighborhoods having to deal with what's going on in the streets.

It is a mandate for leaders to lead. Leader, you're in that place because God has called you. And since He has called you, He has equipped you, whether you feel equipped or not. God is holding you accountable for leading your people. So leader, this will require that you dive in more deeply: Look at your relationships, look at your dinner table, your board of directors, your elder board, your congregation. But it may also mean you can't find diversity in any of those places, so you'll have to seek out help for yourself and find people who are different from you so you can challenge each other. This is a reach-across situation. The people you find must not be impressed with your degrees or large congregation. You must be able to tell each other the truth.

Leadership is to climate what a thermostat is to temperature; climate determines what grows. Whatever you want to see grow is determined by the seed you plant. And by the way, do you have a white Jesus on your walls? That is propaganda. It's impossible to hide a blond-haired, blue-eyed baby in Egypt, which is in Africa. Leaders have to get honest about both American history and biblical history.

### Embrace Your Role and Ask for Help

It's important to know whether you are the leader who speaks the language of Christocentrism/ethnoconsciousness well enough for your people to be able to follow you in this venture. You are not a failure if you are not fluent here. Find someone you can get behind and recommend that your people follow that person's lead in this area. You can sit down and join your people in learning. Having them watch you follow is also leadership.

## The Change Sequence, Step Two: Repent

Have you noticed that the majority of the people who are storming the streets with the message that something must be done about racism are black people and other people of color? I'm not going to let my white brothers and sisters off the hook. Just because the negative ramifications of racism don't seem to affect you, that doesn't mean it's okay for you to do nothing about them.

### Recognize the Complexity, Accept Your Complicity, Renew Your Mind

As we've seen in earlier chapters, racism is affecting you too. People who don't look like you are basically asking you to listen—hear and understand the story. Then accept your complicity and renew your mind.

One of the first things we tend to do when we find out we are wrong and need to change is to justify our past behavior. We say, "I did this because of that," or "I acted like that because of this," and on and on. But when we find out that our elders, family members, mentors, and forefathers were wrong, we often try to justify their actions as well, even when as Christians, we know that they were wrong. Never ever justify wrong; wrong is wrong.

Even further, we try to justify sin. Sin is sin whether from Grandma, Grandpa, Uncle or Aunt So-and-So, or Mrs. So-and-So. And sin should always be repented of—no matter the source. We often want to give significant figures in our lives a pass and that is because we want to continue feeling great about them. But we must remember that pedestals are easy to fall off of.

And just because your elder, forefather, or close friends gave you counsel that is inconsistent with God's Word, that doesn't make him or her all bad. Conversely, just because they gave you counsel that was at times consistent with Scripture doesn't make them all good. People are fallible; only God is infallible. If you've heard your dear elder say things about "those people" or that it wasn't okay to date someone because he or she was a "this or that color" (you know what I mean), then the advice without biblical justification is wrong.

Here's the question we must ask ourselves: *Where can I find this comment, suggestion, or opinion in the Bible?* Anything that looks to marginalize people because they don't look like we do, or to discriminate against them because of the color of their skin, or to hate them because of the ethnic group they belong to is sin and is contrary to the Word of God. If you were taught to do so by someone, anyone—an elder in the church, your mother, your father, or an esteemed family friend who has three divinity degrees—that person is wrong. This is what the Bible calls the "counsel of the ungodly." "Blessed is the man who walks not in the counsel of the ungodly, nor stands in the path of sinners, nor sits in the seat of the scornful; but his delight is in the law of the LORD, and in His law he meditates day and night" (Psalm 1:1–2 NKJV).

Racial prejudice is ungodly counsel, a sin. Kevin DeYoung, in a blog post on The Gospel Coalition website, articulated "10 Reasons Racism Is Offensive to God." Citing pertinent Scriptures, DeYoung includes themes already touched on in this book, such as that all people are created in the image of God and that Christians are one in Christ.[1] Additionally, he mentions partiality being a sin, citing the admonition in James 2:1 (NIV): "My brothers and sisters, believers in our glorious Lord Jesus Christ must not show favoritism."[2] His last point, echoing my earlier statement that there is no place in heaven for racism and citing Revelation 5:9–10; 7:9–12; 22:1–5, merits sharing fully here, because I think it is what some people fail to remember most:

> Woe to us if our vision of the good life here on earth will be completely undone by the reality of new heavens and new earth yet to come. Antagonism toward people of another color, language, or ethnic background is antagonism toward God himself and his design for eternity. Christians ought to reject racism, and do what they

> can to expose it and bring the gospel to bear upon it, not because we love pats on the back for our moral outrage or are desperate for restored moral authority, but because we love God and submit ourselves to the authority of his word.[3]

This is why repentance is critical to a successful change sequence.

When someone mentions repentance, the action of showing sincere regret or remorse, many people think of the Old Testament. The picture of someone pitifully dressed in sackcloth and ashes is absolutely valid. It represents someone being sorry or contrite about something he has done, coupled with a commitment to change for the better.

Although both the Old Testament and the New Testament call for significant changes associated with repentance, I think the New Testament definition brings greater clarity. Matthew 4:17 (NKJV) says, "From that time Jesus began to preach, and to say, 'Repent: for the kingdom of heaven is at hand.'" Expanding on what we learned in chapter 5, the Greek translated as "repent" in this verse means "to think differently . . . reconsider (morally to feel compunction)," "to change one's mind for [the] better, heartily to amend with abhorrence of one's past sins."[4] In short, one could say that to repent means to change the way you think.

Romans 12:2 (KJV) further validates this by saying, "And be not conformed to this world: but be ye transformed by the renewing of your mind." In order to *do* differently, we must first *think* differently, but if our intellectual diet consists of watching the same news all the time, and being around the same people who look, think, act, and believe the same way we do, then we can rest assured that our world will get smaller and smaller. Our personal version of the world becomes what we believe to be the actual world to be. This is a recipe for intellectual and spiritual disaster.

When we fold ourselves into the narrow worldview that includes only ourselves and those who agree with us, instead of focusing on simply being the ones for whom Jesus died, we become ethnocentric Christoconscious Christians. We become the individual who bases all our beliefs on our upbringing, ethnicity, and natural culture. This is the core of our identity.

*Well*, I hear you saying, *what could be wrong with that? Why is it a problem to base personal belief on upbringing, ethnicity, and natural culture?* This is dangerous because it is in this frame of mind that Jesus is simply a good idea or an option, but not Lord. While thinking of Jesus as a good person may lead to a pious life, it will not lead to an eternally powerful life, and this type of powerless Christian life is the fundamental component in the division within the body of Christ that we've examined. The ethnocentric Christoconscious Christian is religious, but not relational. This person is very happy rejoicing in his or her ethnicity and never seeing the need to reach across the aisle. Once we realize we are thus identified, it's time for repentance, time for a radical change in our thinking. We would be characterized as cultural Christians, and there are many, many times when we would stand in direct opposition to the covenant Christian—the Christocentric ethnoconscious Christian—a vastly different representative of the kingdom of God.

### Stop Fearing the Conversation

It's okay for African American brothers and sisters to be more direct with their white brothers and sisters than they might have been in the past because it's time to get this done. We're not beating each other up, we're just ready to grow. Because of our commitment to piety, many of us have just kept quiet, but quiet doesn't mean the problem has disappeared. The division has just gotten worse. Feeling convicted, not condemned, is a good thing.

### Conversation Dissolves Stereotypes

When we have conversations, not fearing to ask and answer questions even about subjects that seem taboo, we will find that we are speaking with another human being. The stuff we were taught about each other will dissolve when we can just speak as people to each other. Transparency and vulnerability are necessary to build relationships. Get one on one. We are going to have to manufacture some moments to get conversation going.

### Get Off the Sidelines

Why is the church the last one in the conversation? The church should be leading this conversation, which is going on whether the church is a part of it or not. In my corporate world, companies are talking about this, writing policies, etc., but the church is quiet. We can't seem to get over our politics and denominations to get to the person on the other side. We can't blame culture for what it is when we are sitting on the sidelines being very quiet yet very judgmental. Don't complain about what you permit. Either shut up and let things happen as they are happening or get involved and be a part of the solution.

We think of repentance in a limited way. What does walking in a new way look like? It looks like the one-on-ones. It looks like the conversations in the barbershop. It looks like black people no longer rescuing white people from having epiphanies—those are all actions of repentance. Repentance manifests in action. "For as the body without the spirit is dead, so faith without works is dead also" (James 2:26 KJV). Saying "I'm not a racist" means nothing without proof. You cannot say you have repented and then act the same way you did before. There must be corresponding action. That's why the Bible says we will know the tree by the fruit it bears: "You will know them by their fruits" (Matthew 7:16 NKJV).

## The Change Sequence, Step Three: Redefine

To redefine is to explain again or differently. Luke 11:24–26 (NIV) states that "when an impure spirit comes out of a person, it goes through arid places seeking rest and does not find it. Then it says,

'I will return to the house I left.' When it arrives, it finds the house swept clean and put in order. Then it goes and takes seven other spirits more wicked than itself, and they go in and live there. And the final condition of that person is worse than the first." Essentially, once we have gotten rid of what I call *stinkin' thinkin'* by repenting or changing the way we think about people of different ethnicities and cultures, if we don't fill the vacuum, something else or someone else will.

Redefining is only half of the work. We must also replace the old knowledge with the new or refill the void left by getting rid of our old way of thinking. If we don't, we have not allowed the Holy Spirit to do a thorough work in us.

## Embrace Your Better Self

The Word of God tells us "do not be conformed to this world, but be transformed by the renewing of your mind, that you may prove what is that good and acceptable and perfect will of God" (Romans 12:2 NKJV). We must replace old with new, secular with sacred, ethnocentric rhetoric with Christocentric wisdom. As Jesus said, you don't put "new wine into old wineskins" (Mark 2:22).

A dear friend, who I consider to be a leader of leaders, told me that when he surrendered himself to this process, for a time he felt as though he was in an identity free fall. Much of who he was conditioned to be and thought he was through some of his upbringing was brought into question. And when compared with the Word of God, the advice from some of the dearest elders in his life was flat-out wrong. He had to reconcile the disparity between what he had been taught and what he was learning because the difference changed everything. His commitment to God's Word redefining his identity is why I think he is such an amazing, God-honoring individual, and he is still someone I consider a best friend. He understood that he could still love and honor those elders, but he had to replace their counsel with God's.

## A Christocentric Redefining

Of course, this work of the Spirit of God in our hearts is ongoing; we never arrive. Even in our best moments, we are still a work in progress. The first thing to do is ask God, "Fix *me*," instead of taking the approach that you are going to fix the division between the races/ethnicities. I even heard another leader describe it as feeling like he was born again—again. This change sequence is no small thing; it goes to our core. You may feel as though your house of identity is being stripped down to the studs. That is exactly what is being done and is why this journey is not for the faint of heart. Psalm 127:1–2 (NKJV) says, "Unless the Lord builds the house, they labor in vain who build it; unless the Lord guards the city, the watchman stays awake in vain. It is vain for you to rise up early, to sit up late, to eat the bread of sorrows; for so He gives His beloved sleep."

Notice in this passage that God never asked us to build the house; that's His job. God has asked us to rest, walk and believe. Because the act of trying to do a job that only God has the ability to do only ends up causing us stress, strain, and frustration. This is work that we cannot do without God. In other words, politics can't do it, denominationalism can't do it, and neither can our ethnicity, birth order, gender, or financial strength. This house can't be purchased with money. It can only be secured by surrendering to the One who has the blueprint, Jesus. We are to lay down our lives and pick up His, which includes reprioritizing our earthly identity by moving it out of first place. And it is only by trusting God enough to do so that we can find ourselves: "Whoever loves father or mother more than me is not worthy of me; and whoever loves son or daughter more than me is not worthy of me; and whoever does not take up the cross and follow me is not worthy of me. Those who find their life will lose it, and those who lose their life for my sake will find it" (Matthew 10:37–39 NRSV).

## Dare to Be Vulnerable

A great place to start when embarking upon mind renewal is 1 John 4:20 (AMP) which states, "If anyone says, 'I love God,' and hates (works against) his [Christian] brother, he is a liar; for the one who does not love his brother whom he has seen, cannot love God whom he has not seen." But wait, there's more! You may be thinking, *I don't hate my brothers and sisters who are different from me*. Are you sure? Your definition of hate and God's may differ. And if they do, guess whose definition has to change? Hint: not God's.

You see, God's definition gets to the subtleties of what *hate* actually is. Hate is not simply about wearing a white hood over your head or burning a cross in someone's yard. According to 1 John 4:20, *hate* means to love less. That should cast this entire mindset in a different light. God's Word is not even talking about the open, aggressive, mean-spirited, sometimes violent manifestation of what we know hate to be. It's talking about what are called microaggressions.

I saw a great article on *BuzzFeed* entitled "21 Racial Microaggressions You Hear on a Daily Basis." The website explains the term *microaggression* (originally coined in the 1970s), as used by Columbia professor Derald Wing Sue to refer to "brief and commonplace daily verbal, behavioral, or environmental indignities, whether intentional or unintentional, that communicate hostile, derogatory, or negative racial slights and insults toward people of color."[5]

Let's look at a couple of the insults listed in the article that we may be guilty of allowing to come out of our own mouth:

- "So what does your HAIR look like today? . . . as she pulled off my hat. . . ."
- "So . . . you're Chinese . . . right?"[6]

And here are a few more I have heard—you may have too, as the offender or the offended:

- "I don't see you as black."
- "What *are* you, really?"
- "So, what do you guys speak down there? Mexican?"
- "Really? You listen to country music? Weird!"
- "You're pretty, for a dark-skinned girl."
- "You sound white."

You get the point.

### Unity Commands the Blessing

People who redefine how they think, feel, and act toward people who are different from them have to do serious work; they need a spiritual reprogramming, if you will. Callousness is a hard-heart condition. A soft heart is one that is willing to change. People must ask themselves some fundamental and sobering questions:

Why do I have such discomfort or disdain for someone with whom God is completely comfortable?

Why do I have such a problem with people who don't look like me when I know they are made in the image of God, just like me?

Why am I most comfortable with people who look like me?

When was the last time I had a meal with someone who was different from me?

These questions will help each of us as we begin our journey to redefine our way of thinking as we bring it into greater alignment with the way God thinks about color and ethnicity. Our Father God, who is perfect, tells us to break bread together at the table of blessing because He knows there is healing at that table. Nothing God tells us to do will damage us—all He requires of us is for our good.

"Behold, how good and how pleasant it is for brethren to dwell together in unity," Psalm 133:1 (NKJV) says. It takes maturity to live in unity, and God commands a blessing there. To bless means to empower to prosper. Satan fights so hard against this because he knows we will be closer to God and therefore much more powerful if we are unified. The division between us is indeed satanic.

In our final chapter, we'll look at the final stages of the change sequence and a model for reconciliation, recompense, and restoration.

## Closing the Fracture

1. As a white person, what is one thing you have always wanted to ask a black person?
2. As a black person, what is one thing you always wanted to ask a white person?
3. As a white person, what is one thing you always wanted to tell a black person?
4. As a black person, what is one thing you always wanted to tell a white person?
5. As a white person, what is one stereotype about black people you hold?
6. As a black person, what is one stereotype about white people you hold?
7. If you are a white leader, how will you introduce the need for diversity, conciliation, and reconciliation to your congregation, family, company, or community?

## Chapter Glossary of Terms

**Microaggression**—"A subtle but offensive comment or action directed at a member of a marginalized group, especially a racial minority, that is often unintentionally offensive or unconsciously reinforces a stereotype." Also, "discriminating against a marginalized group by means of such comments or actions."[7]

# Adopt the Change Model

Peace is priceless. You can't buy it because real peace can only come from the Prince of Peace. Peace isn't the absence of conflict but calm in the midst of it. Only the Lord can give that. I am so blessed to be part of the Welch family. One day it dawned on me that we never need a reason to get together; we just love being together, so we'll all end up at a family member's house. I also realized that there is little to no drama in our family. One of the reasons for that is because my grandparents William (Bill) and Catherine (Kitty) Welch considered loving family one of the highest priorities, especially between the siblings. If a cross word was spoken from one family member to another, you had better get it right, right away. Of course, this wasn't to say that ours was a perfect household, none is. But getting along, loving each other, and apologizing to each other if there had been disrespect or disregard for someone's feelings were of paramount importance, or you could count on receiving discipline of some sort.

That's why today my mom's generation—my aunts and my uncles—adore each other. Their love is real, not show. Anyone who knows our family knows love, honor, compassion, and unity are our guiding forces—our non-negotiables. And this is why we have so many surrogate members. The amazing men and women who married into our family operate in the same fashion. Quite simply, they are some of the most noble and honorable people I know.

This is the cloth from which I am cut. Thank you, Lord, for this priceless gift.

Coming from this background gives me a deeper understanding of reconciliation. There is nothing I would do intentionally to cause strife, discord, or drama within my family because of the peace in which I've been raised and the supernatural value of it. I'm not saying we're perfect, but when there is even slight tension between family members, which is very rare, we run toward reconciliation. Why? Because of the value, and more important, the history of the friendship that exists between the individuals. We didn't ride on this boat together this long with each other only to abandon ship. That cost would be just too great.

## The Change Sequence, Step Four: Reconcile

So let's go on to implement what we have learned. Now, when I take the same principles from the Welch family, my earthly family, and apply them to the family of God, my heavenly family, and the reconciliation that we always talk about in church services, I am sorry to say that I think we have the cart before the horse. Many of us haven't invested time, tears, life, or a truly listening ear to really be friends. Events such as reconciliation services won't get us where we need to be. Those kinds of services (or events) have a value because they are movements in the right direction but are only part of the answer.

### The Development of True and Authentic Friendships

Remember, it has been stated before. In order to reconcile, you have to have been friends before. Reconciliation has become an event rather than a lifestyle. How are you really going to act after you leave the foot-washing service? Are you really going to go back into your office, your church, and your community and be a change agent? Be a friend based upon what someone needs, not upon what you think they need. And you cannot be a friend without doing the hard work to build the relationship—the hard work it takes to really listen and get to know someone.

Our Heavenly Father demands unity. We tend to demand *uniformity*. Diversity is God's idea, and true unity can't happen without diversity. Unity can only be expressed by the coming together of things that at one point in time were not unified because of their differences. There is no miracle of unity when everybody in the room is already alike in almost every way possible. The miracle of unity is when people from every tribe, nation, and tongue unify as one tribe. That's a miracle. So if we've not taken the time to first build a friendship and a history with one another, what is there to reconcile?

No wonder I've heard more than a few people say, "Reconcile about what? I didn't even know anything was wrong!" Such questions and comments are pervasive in many circles throughout the body of Christ because there is very little understanding of shared history. That gives birth to many friendships that, at best, are cordial, pleasant, or politically correct. I am not dismissing the few friendships that are deep, but those take unfiltered honesty, transparency, shared history and experience, occasional disagreements, and arguments. Nevertheless, they also take an unwavering commitment to always come back to the table of fellowship. These types of friendships, though they certainly exist, are rare.

I've also heard people ask, "So what's the endgame of all this reconciliation talk?" "What is our 'why'?" "What is my return on investment for this?" Really? The endgame is ongoing relationship. We are not just in this to have an event and move on. Understanding the need for diversity and reaching the reconciliation of the races/ethnicities *is* the point.

### Cultivate Diverse Friendships

We should all have friends from different walks of life and with outlooks different from our own. We don't have to agree with people to love them. Thinking through diverse thoughts helps us crystalize our own beliefs. An agenda shouldn't even be a part of the conversation. We aren't building relationships to sell something; we're simply building relationships because people are intrinsically valuable. This familiar instruction attributed to St. Francis of Assisi, "Preach the Gospel at all times and when necessary, use words," is directed at Christians. We are not being disobedient to the Great Commission if every conversation does not end with a prayer to receive Christ. Just be a friend.

### Assessing Relationships

When the deception and idol of white superiority and privilege meets the deception and idol of black or person of color inferiority, the intersection is not a friendship in which Christ is at the center. This, rather, is a friendship of the blind leading the blind as both are deceived but in different ways. Simply because of the color of their skin, members of one side are deceived into thinking they are better and privileged; members of the other are deceived into thinking they are lesser and disadvantaged. This is a losing formula and an incorrect framework.

The correct framework is a kingdom framework in which both sides find their sufficiency in Christ. They then must both use what they have been given to help the other realize their purpose and calling for the kingdom. Perhaps the help would entail the sharing of each other's network, finances, insight, or maybe a listening ear. This kingdom friendship must tear down every wall that limits and separates. A unity must be allowed to emerge that is not based on an ethnic group, denomination, or any of the other things we have allowed to become walls. This unity must be intentional and strategic in articulating something different. Different to the principalities and powers of the air that declare and manifest the devil's greatest nightmare: unity manifesting God's covenant family based on the blood of Jesus. This unity is as much a weapon against the kingdom of darkness as it is a joy for those involved in it.

Christocentric relationships are transformational. When you have redefined your framework, you might look around and see that some of the relationships you already have are pretty superficial. One price you may pay is in the friends you lose because they weren't really friends in the first place. When you have this new orientation around a Christocentric identity, and that begins to come out of your mouth because it's in your heart now, you might find the people you were previously connected to may start to back away from you. People are not your friends if they will stop loving you because they disagree with you. The payoff is that you are now going to be introduced to family and a much richer sense of what family means. Would you rather stay in transactional relationships, or would you rather move up to transformational relationships? An ethnocentric relationship can only end up in transaction, but a Christocentric relationship is wired for transformation.

Now, caution! Living in this type of unity is where reconciliation or the lack thereof carries a hefty price. We *must* reconcile because if we don't, then our shared history and the supernatural friendship we've built over many years and many tears will never have the opportunity to manifest God's heart for the world to see. This is the deep unity Jesus speaks of that will be a witness to the rest of the world.

> I do not pray for these alone, but also for those who will believe in Me through their word; that they all may be one, as You, Father, are in Me, and I in You; that they also may be one in Us, that the world may believe that You sent Me. And the glory which You gave Me I have given them, that they may be one just as We are one: I in them, and You in Me; that they may be made perfect in one, and

> that the world may know that You have sent Me, and have loved them as You have loved Me.
>
> John 17:20–23 NKJV

Reconciliation is often mentioned within the context of bringing different ethnic groups together, especially within the body of Christ; however, the idea and execution of the idea often miss the mark:

> So, from now on, we refuse to evaluate people merely by their outward appearances. For that's how we once viewed the Anointed One, but no longer do we see him with limited human insight. Now, if anyone is enfolded into Christ, he has become an entirely new person. All that is related to the old order has vanished. Behold, everything is fresh and new. And God has made all things new, and reconciled us to himself, and given us the ministry of reconciling others to God.
>
> 2 Corinthians 5:16–18 TPT

I sometimes struggle with the ministry of reconciliation according to the Word of God being made synonymous with the various efforts that seek to bring people of different ethnicities together, particularly Christians who are African American and European American. This is speaking about reconnecting or "*re*-conciling" the friendship that God had with humans before the fall of Adam. In the beginning, humans and God were in deep fellowship and friendship. Adam and Eve sinned, which broke the beautiful friendship and fellowship they enjoyed. This broken relationship deployed havoc over the entire human race. In the Old Testament, a complicated annual ceremony involving the sacrifice of bulls and goats by the high priest had to happen to satisfy God's wrath against mankind. Let that sink in. Every single year, this ceremony had to take place to ask God yet again to forgive their sins. This is why the shed blood of Jesus and His sacrifice changed everything for everyone. Hebrews 10:4–10 (TPT) makes this clear:

> For what power does the blood of bulls and goats have to remove sin's guilt? So when Jesus the Messiah came into the world he said,
>
> "Since your ultimate desire was not another animal
> sacrifice;
> you have clothed me with a body
> that I might offer myself instead!
> Multiple burnt offerings and sin-offerings
> cannot satisfy your justice.
> So, I said to you, 'God—
> I will be the One to go and do your will,
> to fulfill all that is written of me in your Word!'"
>
> First, he said, "Multiple burnt-offerings and sin-offerings cannot satisfy Your justice" (even though the law required them to be offered).
>
> And then he said, "God, I will be the One to go and do your will." *So by being the sacrifice that removes sin*, he abolishes animal sacrifices and replaces that entire system with the new covenant. By God's will we have been purified and made holy once and for all through the sacrifice of the body of Jesus, the Messiah!

Jesus Christ was the sacrifice that satisfied the wrath of God forever. Although it is up to the individual to accept that sacrifice, the work has been done. This is the ministry of reconciliation of which God is speaking. God was friends with humans; humans sinned, and that friendship was broken. Jesus, who is God who came to earth in bodily form, shed His blood and gave His own life to *re*-concile (or to reestablish the friendship that was broken between humankind and God).

And here is what brings me to my next point: In order to *reconcile*, you must by necessity have been conciliatory or friends previously. Our job as Christians is to reestablish the friendship and relationship that God had in the beginning with humankind, with those who are God's estranged children. This is the ministry of reconciliation.

Repairing the breach between God and humans is very different from repairing the relationships from person to person or church to church.

Again, two people need to have been friends in the first place in order to be friends *again*. If I have a friend who is white (and I have many of them) and we fall out with each other, then we can, by definition, reconcile, because we had a friendship before.

So let's discuss a hard question. When have African Americans ever had a true friendship with our nation? Our history doesn't suggest that there has ever been a deep and abiding friendship between African Americans and America. Too many statistics in too many industries and in too many areas substantially support this assertion.

Let me ask another question: What are we actually doing in the body of Christ between the various ethnicities? As we try to work together, show love toward each other, and act more like the family of God as God defines it, are we actually involved in *conciliation* and not *reconciliation*? In other words, aren't we really involved in the work of *becoming* friends rather than reestablishing a friendship?

We must still face it: Civil rights icon Rev. Dr. Martin Luther King Jr. was right when he said that "11 o'clock on Sunday morning is one of the most segregated hours, if not *the* most segregated hours in Christian America."[1] The reason we continually quote these words is because we are still so very segregated and, for the most part, we're okay with it.

This comfort, this complacency with being separate, actually underscores our immaturity as Christians. The vast majority of Christians would rather fellowship with, go to church with, be friends with, vacation with, break bread with, invest in business with, live in neighborhoods with, and spend time with other Christians who are most "like" themselves. This is immaturity on steroids. Hence, I think we are doing the right thing, but calling it the wrong thing. God has given us the ministry of reconciliation as we reconnect lost men and women back to the God who passionately loves them, while we, as maturing sons and daughters of God, become the friends to each other that God intended for God's family to be in the first place. John 17:21 (TPT) says, "I pray for them all to be joined together as one even as you and I, Father, are joined together as one. I pray for them to become one with us so that the world will recognize that you sent me."

The Word of God also says:

> How wonderful and pleasant it is
>     when brothers live together in harmony!
> For harmony is as precious as the anointing oil
>     that was poured over Aaron's head
>     that ran down his beard
>     and onto the border of his robe.
> Harmony is as refreshing as the dew from Mount Hermon
>     that falls on the mountains of Zion.
> And there the Lord has pronounced his blessing
>     even life everlasting.
>
> Psalm 133

Yes, it's about time that we—all the members of the body of Christ no matter what color, whatever amount of melanin—actually become friends. Before we can reconcile, we must first "concile." (Yes, I made up that word, but you get the point.)

## The Change Sequence, Stage Five: Recompense

At the conclusion of a recent talk I gave to an auditorium filled with Christian business people, someone in the audience commented that they wanted their city to be known for its virtue of being a holy city. I responded that though the title is admirable, "I think a better witness would be for *visitors* to this amazing city to call it a holy city from what they observed, not from what marketing materials stated. Let them see your witness in how you treat each other, especially across ethnic lines." This was an especially intentional comment because this particular city was very much involved in the US slave trade.

What I find so remarkable and powerful is that the mayor, along with quite a number of other committed members of the family of God, is stepping up and confronting the city's slaveholding past, offering written apologies, giving public repentances, and working diligently to honor God by being honest. At the end of my talk, during the Q & A, another member of the audience asked me what they should do next to show they are serious about their repentance as a community. I responded that because their community was made economically strong by its early involvement in the slave trade, it made sense that the most visible sign of their repentance would also be in the marketplace. Making amends with someone because of loss or harm suffered necessitates compensation.

*So, Skot, are you talking about reparations?* Yup. There is a need to recognize that it's time to do something to make this right. The Scripture even gives an example of this when the Israelites were freed from bondage in Egypt. The Egyptians gave them gold, clothing, etc. before the slaves left. Recompense (or restitution, reparations) is a fundamental component of true repentance as well as biblical justice. Actually, recompense must be a part of every repentance where economic damage and/or harm has been done to a community of people. The principle is seen in the book of Exodus 12: 31–36 (NKJV):

> Then he called for Moses and Aaron by night, and said, "Rise, go out from among my people, both you and the children of Israel. And go, serve the LORD as you have said. Also take your

> flocks and your herds, as you have said, and be gone; and bless me also."
>
> And the Egyptians urged the people, that they might send them out of the land in haste. For they said, "We shall all be dead." So the people took their dough before it was leavened, having their kneading bowls bound up in their clothes on their shoulders. Now the children of Israel had done according to the word of Moses, and they had asked from the Egyptians articles of silver, articles of gold, and clothing. And the LORD had given the people favor in the sight of the Egyptians, so that they granted them what they requested. Thus they plundered the Egyptians.

Psalm 105:37 (NKJV) also speaks of this principle, looking at the same event:

> He also brought them out with silver and gold,
> And *there was* none feeble among His tribes.

It needs to be clearly understood that something has been stolen from African Americans. They were stolen from their continent and countries. Their heritage was stolen from them. Their culture was stolen from them. Then over the years here in America, when their predecessors started building any kind of wealth, dignity, and position, those things were also summarily stolen over and over again.

## God's Economy: Diverse, Creative, and Collaborative

America has to come to terms with the reality that our economy was built on almost 250 years of free labor, and you can't call that biblical. Our country was built on human trafficking. We lack intellectual and spiritual integrity not to admit this.

With that thought in mind, I suggested that the local business leaders, along with the city, start an investment or venture fund of some sort to which entrepreneurs would have access to investment dollars for the start-up of their businesses or for accessing additional capital for taking their businesses to the next level. I could feel the room get very still, but I continued with my thought, and I think some of them came around. I further stated that there can be no real repentance as it relates to trying to mend past atrocities without some sort of compensation. Financial compensation.

The room remained silent as I added the clincher to my suggestion. I told them to make the capital accessible to those start-up entrepreneurs' businesses given that they passed the viability test—but to add one more requirement (and this would be a deal breaker). I suggested that part of the criteria for accessing the capital be that the equity-ownership and senior leadership team be a multiethnic team. Oftentimes, people love their money more than they love humanity and this would be at least one way to test whether or not that was true of the people involved. People take their money very personally, but I think it's funny how people act as if they love God until their actual god, *mammon* (money), shows up and tells them to bow at his altar of worship. This is where, as they say, the rubber meets the road.

I believe that in order to fix the overtly biased climate in which the church continues to be so splintered, we, as the family of God, must honestly and transparently come to terms with our sordid history. Yes, the American church was complicit in the structuring of what was known as "the peculiar institution" of slavery.

> Though slavery was used openly in the past by ancient cultures to create wealth, it is today regarded as an act of injustice against humanity. The trans-Atlantic slave trade between the fifteenth and nineteenth centuries is no exception. Christians who claimed to have the love of God and humanity at the centre of their religion were involved in slavery's atrocious trade practices to create wealth. The church's involvement in this economic venture seems paradoxical and contrary to its mission of love for all humanity. . . .

> In the wake of the independence of the United States of America in 1776, there was agitation for the end of slavery in the new nation that was met with opposition. Some denominations began to take measures against slavery, with the Quakers expelling from their midst those who insisted on holding slaves in 1776, and the American Methodists and the Baptists banning slaveholding among their members. . . . Some denominations remained indecisive on the issue to end slavery. The General Assembly of the Presbyterian Church in 1818, for instance, declared that slavery was against the law of God, but opposed its abolition. The Catholic Jesuits did not tolerate slavery and did not want slaves in their settlements.[2]

The shadow of slavery still influences every other system in our great nation and world. From financial systems to corporate structures to healthcare to education to the judicial system to neighborhoods, and so on, every system in the great United States of America has been infected by the disease of slavery.

There also are more modern day, secular examples of our how our early US economy boomed specifically because of slavery. I found an article written from a Jewish perspective to be particularly interesting. In his article "The Torah Case for Reparations," Aryeh Bernstein states,

> Rabbi Shmuly Yanklowitz began to point toward an argument for reparations from Jewish texts and this past Rosh HaShana, Rabbi Sharon Brous delivered a searing sermon, later condensed and published in the *Los Angeles Times*, calling for Jewish support for reparations to Black Americans, summoning a famous, early Talmudic teaching in which the Schools of Hillel and Shammai dispute the *method* of making restitution when a stolen beam is built into the foundation of a house, but agree that restitution must be made (Talmud Bavli Gittin 55a). "Our country was built on a stolen beam," preached Rabbi Brous. "Except it was several

> million stolen beams. And they weren't beams; they were human beings." . . .
>
> Jews must support reparations in principle, because we took reparations for our slave labor, we were commanded by God to do so, and we were promised these reparations in the earliest Divine plan for our liberation. Let us review our Scriptures.[3]

In her article entitled "The Clear Connection Between Slavery and American Capitalism," Dina Gerdeman writes that in exploring the ties between slavery and nineteenth-century economic development in the 2016 book *Slavery's Capitalism: A New History of American Economic Development*, sixteen scholars are "helping to set the record straight."

> The small farmers of New England weren't alone responsible for establishing America's economic position. . . . Rather, the hard labor of slaves in places like Alabama, South Carolina, and Mississippi needs to be kept in view as well. . . . More than half of the nation's exports in the first six decades of the 19th century consisted of raw cotton, almost all of it grown by slaves. . . .
>
> The slave economy of the southern states had ripple effects throughout the entire U.S. economy, with plenty of merchants in New York City, Boston, and elsewhere helping to organize the trade of slave-grown agricultural commodities—and enjoying plenty of riches as a result.
>
> "In the decades between the American Revolution and the Civil War, slavery—as a source of the cotton that fed Rhode Island's mills, as a source of the wealth that filled New York's banks, [and] as a source of the markets that inspired Massachusetts manufacturers—proved indispensable to national economic development," [editors] Beckert and Rockman write.[4]

## Recompense—Lift As You Climb

Wherever you're going as you become more and more enlightened to your reconciliation responsibility, reach back and pull someone else up to go with you. Ed Silvoso, a wonderful Argentinian evangelist and author, has said that the health of a community can be seen by the inequity or the equity in its marketplace. There could be beautiful streets and homes, but if there is inequity in the marketplace, you're looking at a sick city. So when we talk about the economics of it and the coming together in the spirit of recompense, there's so much we can do. Everything we do as Christians is redemptive in nature. If we could come together, we could actually redeem an economy. We would shift not only the economic landscape of the community, but also the spiritual landscape of the community.

As we continue this discussion, an extremely pertinent question to ask at this juncture is what system has *not* been adversely affected by our involvement in the trafficking of human souls?

The problem we face is not just that slavery and its residual effects are wrong, it's that the people whom God calls His family—even when people don't—helped to put the system in place, with many of those people insisting that it was God's will.

We, as Christians from all walks of life, must have the tough conversations about the true harm suffered by Christians of color, not just in the US but around the world. Yes, it will be uncomfortable, but I believe that is one of the most fundamental roles the Comforter should play in every Christian's life: to help us to become comfortable in uncomfortable conversations and situations. He's ready. Are we? I actually think so. In fact, I think this is our opportunity. And if you think that the need to have this conversation will go away if we just wait it out, you're wrong. God will wait us out. And I believe that we will miss out on what is the catalyst conversation for one of the biggest outpourings of God's Spirit in history. This is an opportunity, not an issue. It's an opportunity for *now*.

The Hebrew word for work—*avodah*—also means worship and service. As we work together and serve each other, we are worshiping God.

## The Change Sequence, Step Six: Restore

### To Return Something to a Former Owner, Place, or Condition

Family, if we can get this right, I believe God would do something so powerfully fresh and new that we would see people come to Christ in numbers we have never before seen. It takes mature Christians to love each other as God desires for us to love each other. But we will have to pick up the ministry of the Christocentric ethnoconscious Christian and lay down, even forsake, the lifestyle of the ethnocentric Christoconscious religious person. Remember, it was the religious community that crucified Jesus. That's not the side we want to be on.

"So, because Jesus was doing these things on the Sabbath, the Jewish leaders began to persecute him. In his defense Jesus said to them, 'My Father is always at his work to this very day, and I too am working.' For this reason, they tried all the more to kill him; not only was he breaking the Sabbath, but he was even calling God his own Father, making himself equal with God" (John 5:16–18 NIV).

There is a place in God that only true unity can reach. When we are in unity, we look different. We are acting out the Gospel. We do care about each other. God is bringing us to a place where we can be mindful of His heart. And we can't be mindful of it and not want to do something about it. This is where restoration becomes so powerful.

And please understand that I don't believe that we must be uniform to be unified. Again, diversity is God's idea. There are people I can reach for Christ whom you can't; there are people you can reach for Christ whom I can't. The devil knows this. Satan's worst nightmare is when we, as Christians, quit acting like "mere mortals," in the apostle Paul's words of 1 Corinthians 3:3 (NCB). Our unity would awaken a sleeping giant. When we understand who we *really* are and whose we are, we will begin to act differently toward each other. When we begin to live from a place of a

Christocentric ethnoconscious identity, we will begin to experience a grace and power we've never known before.

I'm all in! Are you? If your answer is no, ask the Holy Spirit to reveal to you what's stopping you. God is not expecting you to do this in your own strength. Simply ask God for help. I think that God would answer this prayer quickly. Why? I don't think this is a request that God often gets. He would love to take you through your complete identity transformation. God knows a better version of you is waiting on the other side of this process.

So again, reconciliation is the cart before the horse. People mean well when they boldly declare the necessity for reconciliation. I agree. There is a desperate need for this to become a reality in the body of Christ if we are to truly experience the blessing of God that makes us attractive to the world. However, I find that while people seem to want to jump at reconciliation, they jump right over the fundamental requirements of it: The parties involved must first have had a friendship, a conciliatory relationship, before they can reconcile.

This is why the apostle Paul speaks about both our being reconciled to God *and* our duty to reconcile humanity to God. God's relationship with Adam was a friendship. Adam and Eve sinned and the fellowship between humankind and God was broken. The birth, death, burial, and resurrection of Jesus reconciled man to God. Reconciliation is only possible if we have first had a friendship, which is why we, the different ethnicities in the body of Christ, must begin by recognizing the history that caused the breach in the first place. Then we must build conciliatory relationships with each other across ethnic lines before we can reconcile; otherwise, there can be no true reconciliation.

Let's visit the model and steps to begin.

## Adopting the Change Model

I've worked in the field of diversity, equity, and inclusion for over twenty-five years now and have helped many domestic and global organizations develop metric-based, sustainable processes and systems that transform the workforce, as well as help them more deeply engage their customers, congregants, and clients. It should be noted that having worked with some of the biggest brands during my tenure with a well-known diversity and inclusion magazine, I have just recently started to get requests to work with churches and other faith-based organizations. I'm really excited about this because a heartfelt desire of mine has always been to help the family—other Christians.

I believe that we, as the body of Christ, should be leading the way in the areas of inclusion and understanding diversity, but we are not. Our lagging behind in these areas has everything to do with secular culture seeing a double standard in our behavior. One hand preaches love and unity while the other hand operates as the most segregated and divided population on the planet. We stand on the brink of a great opportunity. We can allow our unity to become the biggest witness of the reality of Christ the world has ever seen. We can bring back a Christian praise chorus of years ago and make it real that "they'll know we are Christians by our love [one to another]."[5]

Remember, we cannot restore our relationships with each other until we restore our relationship with God. God's original intent was for His kids to live in community with each other. We don't realize that it's not home to adopt a political tribe, an ethnic tribe, or a denominational tribe. God wants to call us to our true home—He IS home. Part of God's restoration is always to come back home.

In the appendix of this book, I have included some resources that my firm, Global Bridgebuilders, uses to help our clients develop sustainable diversity and inclusion initiatives that are biblically sound and organizationally transformational.

Since diversity is God's idea, our practice of honoring it honors Him and reflects His heart that His children come together, becoming one. "Hear, O Israel: The LORD our God, the LORD is one" (Deuteronomy 6:4 NKJV). There have been many perspectives shared about this particular verse; however, what it clearly indicates is that unity is inextricably linked to the character of our heavenly Father. The Father, the Son, and the Holy Spirit, although distinct in their roles, are all God and all one. That's a powerful reality. It would be even more powerful if we, as His children, manifested this same unity.

In short, here's what must be done:

**Recognition of the past.** Many people haven't done any historical study about what took place in the past, particularly as it relates to communities of color.

**Repentance.** Once a person has at least some understanding of that past, a change in thinking and subsequently a change in behavior must take place. In other words, there must be visible evidence that a transformation of mind and heart has occurred. True repentance always has fruit.

**Redefinition.** Get rid of *stinkin' thinkin'* by repenting or changing the way we think about people of different ethnicities and cultures.

**Reconciliation.** It is in this stage that authentic, transparent, and intentional relationships are built. These relationships are built on the basis of equality. No person is greater or lesser. These are what my dear friend and former pastor Scott Hagan calls "reaching across" relationships instead of "reaching down." Notice that this is not the first step but the third step. You may even be able to think of more steps that are necessary before the final goal is reached.

**Recompense.** Take responsibility for the economic renumeration of those who have been hurt and commit to do the work of making it right financially. This is where the spirit and service of mammon or of our heavenly Father will clearly be seen. Repentance, true repentance, is seen in actions, not simply in words. This must be made right before God.

**Restoration.** It is not until the preceding steps—recognition, repentance, redefinition, reconciliation, and recompense—happen that we are truly able to see restoration take place. And to what are we restored? Our relationships are restored to God's original intention of what fellowship between God's children should truly look like according to His Word, not according to our level of comfort.

Here is a biblical example of what restoration looks like:

> But a prophet of the Lord named Oded was there in Samaria when the army of Israel returned home. He went out to meet them and said, "The LORD, the God of your ancestors, was angry with Judah and let you defeat them. But you have gone too far, killing them without mercy, and all heaven is disturbed. And now you are planning to make slaves of these people from Judah and Jerusalem. What about your own sins against the LORD your God? Listen to me and return these prisoners you have taken, *for they are your own relatives.* Watch out, because now the Lord's fierce anger has been turned against you!"
>
> . . . So, the warriors released the prisoners and handed over the plunder in the sight of the leaders and all the people. Then the four men just mentioned by name came forward and distributed clothes from the plunder to the prisoners who were naked. They provided clothing and sandals to wear, gave them enough food and drink, and dressed their wounds with olive oil. They put those who were weak on donkeys and took all the prisoners back to their own people in Jericho, the city of palms. Then they returned to Samaria.
>
> 2 Chronicles 28:9–11, 14–15, emphasis added

Notice that God's form of reconciliation demands recompense. Now a word about denominationalism.

We are so much more than titles. We are God's family. And while that sounds like a warm and fuzzy observation, I bring it up as an obligation undergirded by a mandate from God. God didn't suggest that we love one another; God commanded us to do so. And we are not to love one another just in theory or simply as an intellectual exercise, but in real, solid, palpable action. John 17:20–26 (NIV) makes it very clear:

> My prayer is not for them alone. I pray also for those who will believe in me through their message, that all of them may be one, Father, just as you are in me and I am in you. May they also be in us so that the world may believe that you have sent me. I have given them the glory that you gave me, that they may be one as we are one—I in them and you in me—so that they may be brought to complete unity. Then the world will know that you sent me and have loved them even as you have loved me.
>
> Father, I want those you have given me to be with me where I am, and to see my glory, the glory you have given me because you loved me before the creation of the world.
>
> Righteous Father, though the world does not know you, I know you, and they know that you have sent me. I have made you known to them, and will continue to make you known in order that the love you have for me may be in them and that I myself may be in them.

The question often arises, how? "So Skot, what do we do to change?" The first thing to do is to ask God to examine our heart and help us to better understand our motives. Why do we want to change? Are we truly committed to systemic change?

It's important to understand that this decision to change will cost us something. I've heard about pastors who get cold feet when it comes to encouraging their congregations to make the necessary changes to reconcile. Those pastors do a dance I call tiptoeing through the tithers. This happens when the notion of self-preservation and the fear of offending the biggest congregational givers kicks in strong. And while I understand why that might be a natural response, it is not a spiritual one. Now I know some may not want to hear my next statement but here goes: This tiptoeing communicates that those pastors are more tied into humans as their source than they are into trusting God as their Source. What if giving goes down because of the proposed, new, purposeful strategy toward true reconciliation? Most likely it will. In fact, when pastors decide to move toward reconciliation, they will probably see sides of some of their congregants that they never knew existed.

I heard one globally recognized pastor say that the strongest pushback he's ever experienced came about as a result of his trying to make this very important change. He personally told me this through tears. Does the difficulty of this path give us permission to opt out? Absolutely not. Consider the following Bible verses on the subject:

- I appeal to you, brothers and sisters, in the name of our Lord Jesus Christ, that all of you agree with one another in what you say and that there be no divisions among you, but that you be perfectly united in mind and thought. (1 Corinthians 1:10 NIV)

- Now these are the gifts Christ gave to the church: the apostles, the prophets, the evangelists, and the pastors and teachers. Their responsibility is to equip God's people to do his work and build up the church, the body of Christ. This will continue until we all come to such unity in our faith and knowledge of God's Son that we will be mature in the Lord, measuring up to the full and complete standard of Christ. (Ephesians 4:11–13)

- Make allowance for each other's faults, and forgive anyone who offends you. Remember, the Lord forgave you, so you must forgive others. Above all, clothe yourselves with love, which binds us all together in perfect harmony. (Colossians 3:13–14)

- How wonderful and pleasant it is when brothers live together in harmony! (Psalm 133:1)

- Finally, all of you should be of one mind. Sympathize with each other. Love each other as brothers and sisters. Be tenderhearted, and keep a humble attitude. (1 Peter 3:8)

- Other verses on the subject include 1 John 4:12; Ephesians 4:3; Romans 12:6; Matthew 23:8; Philippians 2:1; Ephesians 1:10; 2 Chronicles 30:12; Ephesians 2:14; 1 Corinthians 12:12–13; Ephesians 4:16; Romans 6:5.

Although there are more, you get the point. If you can't see God's heart regarding unity and reconciliation by now, your heart is hard. Period. Obtaining unity and the reconciled church are the kingdom imperative.

## Closing the Fracture

1. What can you do to cultivate diverse friendships?
2. Explain why saying "I'm sorry" without some sort of corresponding action is the same as saying you repent without offering recompense. (Recompense and restitution are part of repentance.)
3. How can America consider it honorable to have compensated victims of Japanese internment during World War II, yet deem it unnecessary to offer reparations to descendants of African American slaves who were human

trafficked and then used for nearly 250 years of free, forced labor that built the economy in which many contemporary African Americans have no share?

4. What ideas for reparations can you offer?
5. Who can you reach out to and lift to your current understanding of the need for reconciliation?
6. Are you all in to reach restoration?

## Glossary of Chapter Terms

**Transactional Relationship**—"Refers to a business-like approach to a relationship, where each person in that relationship has clear responsibilities and rewards. Those responsibilities will define what each individual is expected to contribute, as well as the rewards each will receive (or expects to receive) as a result of their efforts. Typical characteristics of transactional relationships include convenience and pre-determined quid pro quo. . . . Additionally, people in transactional relationships tend to be clear on what benefits they will reap from the relationship as well as what is/will be expected from them; expectations are clearly communicated, sometimes even before the relationship begins."[6]

**Reparations**—"Broadly understood as compensation given for an abuse or injury. . . . Reparations are now understood as not only war damages but also compensation and other measures provided to victims of severe human rights violations by the parties responsible. . . . In transitional justice, reparations are measures taken by the state to redress gross and systematic violations of human rights law or humanitarian law through the administration of some form of compensation or restitution to the victims. . . . Reparations, if well designed, acknowledge victims' suffering, offer measures of redress, as well as some form of compensation for the violations suffered. Reparations can be symbolic as well as material. They can be in the form of public acknowledgement of or apology for past violations, indicating state and social commitment to respond to former abuses."[7]

**Recompense**—"To give something to by way of compensation (as for a service rendered or damage incurred)," "to pay for." Also, "to return in kind: requite."[8]

# Action Steps

**Phase Descriptions:**

**Please Note** That Logistics/Scheduling of All Phases of the Initiative Are to Be Handled by a Departmental Coordinator/Employee in Collaboration with Global Bridgebuilders (GBB).

## Phase 1. Workplace Diversity Preparation—Assessment and Benchmarking (Deployed in Both Month 1 and Month 24)

Deployment of Online Inclusion Systems Assessment (iSA)—Organization should begin with a comprehensive plan for the development and implementation of a biblically based Diversity, Equity and Inclusion Management System. This initial plan will continue to be tailored to meet the specific needs through the stages of the project. The results of the Inclusion Systems Assessment (iSA) will be used to develop the overall strategy and tactical plan for the execution of the developmental and training services. Biblically based awareness and sensitivity training will also be a part of the targeted workshops and dialogues for employees to provide an orientation to diversity and inclusion and open channels of communication.

**Included in this phase:**

- **Inclusion Systems Assessment (iSA)**
  - *The Five (5) Competency Dimensions to be measured through the iSA are:*
    - *Leadership*
    - *Communications*
    - *Organizational Processes*
    - *External Relationships*
    - *Systems Criteria/Process Management*

## Phase 2. Dialogue Circles, Strategic Planning, and Recommendations

A strategic plan with recommendations will be established to guide our overall efforts based upon findings from dialogue circles conducted with staff and congregants as well as results of the iSA. A tactical diversity and inclusion work plan will then be developed to identify the specific training and consulting activities needed to support the overall strategy.

**Included in this phase:**

- Written report with executive summary including recommendations and observations.
- Focus groups with employees that will provide a qualitative perspective of department employees.
- Debriefing of key individuals and department director on iSA and focus group results.

## Phase 3. Diversity Management and Inclusion Leadership Training

A specific inclusion education module will be customized and provided to support the overall strategy based upon the results of the iSA, focus groups, and the strategic recommendations.

**Included in this phase:**

- Training for departmental employees based upon recommendation—
- 1.5 hours for Leadership.

## Phase 4. Validation, Gap Analysis, Monitoring, and Continuous Improvement

As the diversity system gains traction, it is important to validate the adherence to the established diversity processes. This is done through a re-deployment of the iSA eighteen months after the launch and analysis of the initial iSA. This reassessment allows the organization and management to identify departmental gains as well as challenges and static performance.

**Included in this phase:**

- A post-deployment of the iSA to measure success and/or application of recommendation.

## Phase 5. Diversity Action Council (DAC) Development

- After extensive assessment, benchmarking findings and training, the development of a Diversity Action Council (DAC) takes place to ensure proper development of diversity management plan and improve communication.
- **The purpose of the DAC is to:**
  - Provide solutions-based insight
  - Generate innovative ideas

  - Help diversity management plan gain and maintain sustainable traction
- **Properly implemented, the DAC will:**
  - Improve organizational performance through the encouragement and implementation of employee and team contributions, which ultimately leads to
    1) the organization's ability to better leverage its ministry's congregants;
    2) increased employee morale and productivity through deeper levels of engagement; and
    3) more accurate and timely communication at all levels of the department and organization.

This process, with established milestones, will provide a roadmap for the design and development of training materials. The systems development process can be applied to any aspect of your innovation through inclusion management system.

**Global Bridgebuilders**

*Innovation Through Inclusion®*

| **Multiphase Process*** | |
|---|---|
| Phase I | Global Bridgebuilders proprietary tool:<br>Inclusion Systems Assessment® (iSA) employee online survey—quantitative/organizational |
| Phase II | Dialogue circles—qualitative/individual |
| Phase III | Summary report with actionable recommendations |
| Phase IV | Customized employee development workshops |
| Phase V | Diversity Action Council (DAC) formation/ recalibration |
| Phase VI | Redeployment of iSA, 18–24 months |

*Process developed by Skot Welch, founder, Global Bridgebuilders

## BLUEPRINT FOR SUCCESS

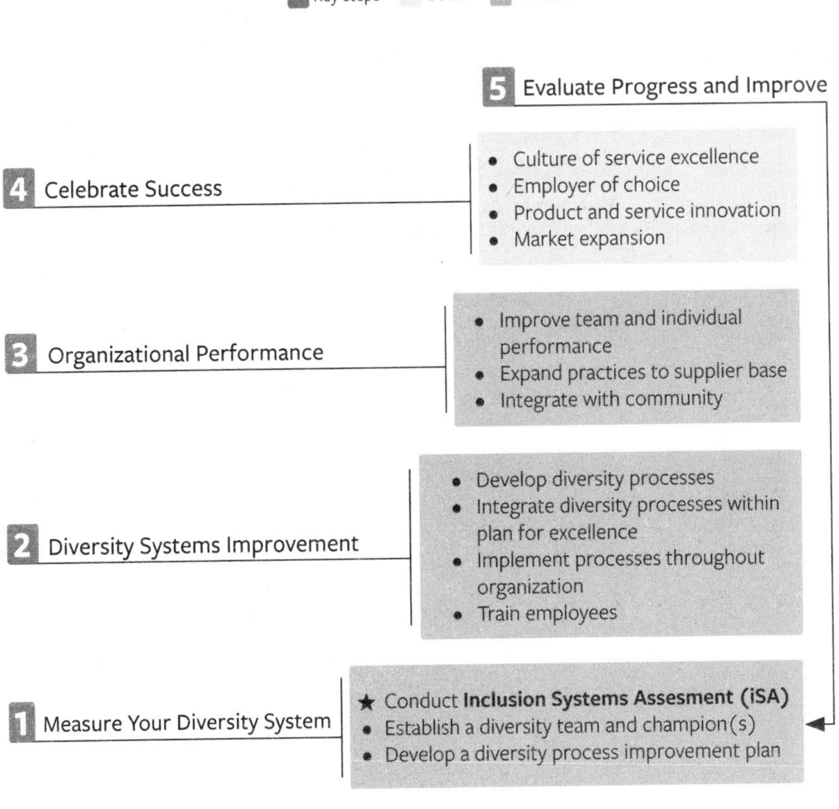


★ **Inclusion Systems Assessment (iSA)** *Developing sustainable organizational diversity processes as part of a successful business strategy*

## Additional Resources (and Sounds)

For resources including an "Unfractured Sonic Landscape" playlist on Spotify, deeper-dive podcasts, as well as information on how to become a certified facilitator of the *Unfractured* curriculum, scan this QR code:

# Notes

## Chapter 1 See False Identities

1. Bertrand Russell, Albert Einstein, et al., "Russell-Einstein Manifesto," issued July 9, 1955, in London, https://ahf.nuclearmuseum.org/ahf/key-documents/russell-einstein-manifesto/.

2. *Merriam-Webster's Unabridged Dictionary*, s.v. "racism," https://unabridged.merriam-webster.com/unabridged/racism.

3. Wikipedia, s.v. "Racism," last updated February 14, 2023, citing Navid Ghani, "Racism," in Richard T. Schaefer, ed., *Encyclopedia of Race, Ethnicity, and Society* (Los Angeles: Sage, 2008), 1113–1115.

4. S. P. Chamberlain, "Recognizing and Responding to Cultural Differences in the Education of Culturally and Linguistically Diverse Learners," *Intervention in School and Clinic* 44, no. 4 (March 2005): 195–211.

5. *Merriam-Webster*, s.v. "mosaic," https://www.merriam-webster.com/dictionary/mosaic.

6. Vivian Hsueh-Hua Chen, "Cultural Identity" in *Key Concepts in Intercultural Dialogue*, no. 22, 2014, https://centerforinterculturaldialogue.files.wordpress.com/2014/07/key-concept-cultural-identity.pdf.

## Chapter 2 Defeat Religious Racism

1. Dr. Martin Luther King Jr. in response to a question during an address at Western Michigan University in Kalamazoo, December 18, 1963.

2. Gwendolyn Seidman, "Why Do We Like People Who Are Similar to Us?," *Psychology Today*, December 18, 2018, https://www.psychologytoday.com/us/blog/close-encounters/201812/why-do-we-people-who-are-similar-us.

3. Seidman, "Why Do We Like People Who Are Similar to Us?"

4. Seidman, "Why Do We Like People Who Are Similar to Us?"

5. Brian McLaren, "The 'Alt-Right' Has Created Alt-Christianity," Patheos, September 18, 2017, https://www.patheos.com/blogs/brianmclaren/2017/09/alt-right-created-alt-christianity/.

6. Curt Landry, "What Is a Religious Spirit?," Curt Landry Ministries, April 5, 2018, https://www.curtlandry.com/what-is-a-religious-spirit/.

7. Peter Lucas Hulen, "Religion," http://persweb.wabash.edu/facstaff/hulenp/religion.html.

8. Kimberly Davis, "The Curious Evangelical Silence over Trayvon Martin," Think Christian, March 23, 2012, https://thinkchristian.net/the-curious-evangelical-silence-over-trayvon-martin.

9. Martin Luther King, "Letter from Birmingham City Jail" in *A Testament of Hope: The Essential Writings and Speeches of Martin Luther King, Jr.*, ed. James Melvin Washington (New York: HarperSanFrancisco, 1986), 300.

10. "Cultural Integrity," Manitoba Arts Council, https://artscouncil.mb.ca/grants/resources/cultural-integrity/.

11. National Park Service, "The Middle Passage," Boston African American National Historic Site, https://www.nps.gov/articles/the-middle-passage.htm.

12. U.S. Department of Labor, "Legal Highlight: The Civil Rights Act of 1964," https://www.dol.gov/agencies/oasam/civil-rights-center/statutes/civil-rights-act-of-1964.

## Chapter 3 Examine Black Culture

1. Cleophus James LaRue, *The Heart of Black Preaching* (Louisville, KY: Westminster John Knox Press, 2000), 1, 6–12.

2. R. Clifford Jones, "African-American Worship: Its Heritage, Character, and Quality," *Ministry*, September 2002, https://www.ministrymagazine.org/archive/2002/09/african-american-worship-its-heritage-character-and-quality.html. Jones cites Frank A. Thomas, *They Like to Never Quit Praisin' God: The Role of Celebration in Preaching* (Cleveland, OH: United Church Press, 1997), 19.

3. Jones, "African-American Worship."

4. Jones, "African-American Worship."

## Chapter 4 Unveil White Culture

1. *Encyclopedia Britannica*, s.v. "African Methodist Episcopal Church," https://www.britannica.com/topic/African-Methodist-Episcopal-Church.

2. Equal Justice Initiative, "White Methodists Exclude Black Clergy in Michigan," On this day—Sep 13, 1907, A History of Racial Injustice Calendar, https://calendar.eji.org/racial-injustice/sep/13.

3. François Bernier, "A New Division of the Earth" from *Journal des Scavans*, April 24, 1684, translated by T. Bendyshe in *Memoirs Read Before the Anthropological Society of London*, vol. 1, 1863–64, 360–64, https://web.archive.org/web/20060524134126/http://www.as.ua.edu/ant/bindon/ant275/reader/bernier.PDF.

4. Carolus Linnaeus, *Systema Naturae*, *Regnum Animale*, 1735, https://www.mun.ca/biology/scarr/4270_Systema_Naturae_1735.html.

5. Johann Friedrich Blumenbach, "On the Natural Variety of Mankind, third ed.," in *The Anthropological Treatises of Blumenbach and Hunter* (London: Longman, Green, Longman, Roberts & Green, 1865), https://blumenbach-online.de/fileadmin/wikiuser/Daten_Digitalisierung/Digitalisate_html/Texte/000010/000010.html#pb145_0001.

6. Raj Bhopal, "The Beautiful Skull and Blumenbach's Errors: The Birth of the Scientific Concept of Race," *British Medical Journal* 335, no. 7633 (December 22, 2007):1308–9.

7. The Higher Education Act of 1965, [P.L. 89–329; Approved November 8, 1965], [As Amended Through P.L. 117–200, Enacted October 11, 2022], https://www.govinfo.gov/content/pkg/COMPS-765/pdf/COMPS-765.pdf.

8. Matt Stefon, "Historically Black Colleges and Universities," *Encyclopedia Britannica*, last updated January 12, 2023, https://www.britannica.com/topic/historically-black-colleges-and-universities.

9. History.com editors, "Harlem Renaissance," *History*, History.com, updated January 22, 2023, https://www.history.com/topics/roaring-twenties/harlem-renaissance.

10. History.com, "Harlem Renaissance."

11. *Merriam-Webster*, s.v. "bigot," https://www.merriam-webster.com/dictionary/bigot.

12. Alexandra Twin, "Disruptive Innovation: Meaning and Examples," Investopedia, updated March 23, 2022, https://www.investopedia.com/terms/d/disruptive-innovation.asp.

**Chapter 5 Build a Bridge to Unity**

1. *Strong's Concordance*, s.v. "3340. metanoeó," Bible Hub, https://biblehub.com/greek/3340.htm.

2. Frederick Douglass, *Narrative of the Life of Frederick Douglass, an American Slave* (Dublin, Ireland: Webb and Chapman, 1846), 118.

3. *The Best of Enemies*, written and directed by Robin Bissell (Universal Pictures Home Entertainment, 2019), DVD.

4. *Merriam-Webster's Unabridged Dictionary*, s.v. "deism," https://unabridged.merriam-webster.com/unabridged/deism.

5. Darren Staloff, "Deism and the Founding of the United States," Divining America, TeacherServe, National Humanities Center, January 2008, https://nationalhumanitiescenter.org/tserve/eighteen/ekeyinfo/deism.htm.

**Chapter 6 Overcome Disunity**

1. Race to Unity, home page, 2019, https://www.racetounity.com/.

2. "The Perils of Groupthink in the Boardroom," Leading Governance, https://leadinggovernance.com/blog/groupthink-in-the-boardroom/.

3. *Strong's Concordance*, s.v. "264. hamartanó," Bible Hub, https://biblehub.com/greek/264.htm.

4. *Thayer's Greek Lexicon,* s.v. "4189. ponéria," Bible Hub, https://biblehub.com/greek/4189.htm.

5. Benjamin Lay, *All Slave Keepers That Keep the Innocent in Bondage* (Philadelphia: printed for the author, 1737), 3–22.

6. Bill Winston, *Vengeance of the Lord* (Bill Winston Ministries, 2019), 1.

7. James Smith as quoted in "Woman Killed Inside Her Home by Fort Worth Officer Was Playing with Her Nephew Moments Before," CBS News DFW, October 12, 2019, https://www.cbsnews.com/dfw/news/woman-killed-inside-her-home-by-fort-worth-officer-was-playing-with-her-nephew-moments-before/.

8. Clayborne Carson, "American Civil Rights Movement," *Encyclopedia Britannica*, last updated January 25, 2023, https://www.britannica.com/event/American-civil-rights-movement.

9. Carson, "American Civil Rights Movement."

10. Carson, "American Civil Rights Movement."

11. Victoria Wilson, "What Is Cultural Identity and Why Is It Important?," Exceptional Futures, 2023, https://www.exceptionalfutures.com/cultural-identity/.

### Chapter 7 Avoid Cultural Ditches

1. William Lloyd Garrison as quoted in Wendell Phillips Garrison and Francis Jackson Garrison, *William Lloyd Garrison, 1805–1879: The Story of His Life Told by His Children*, vol. 3 (Boston: Houghton, Mifflin, 1889), 88.

2. Ani Turner, *The Business Case for Racial Equity* (Battle Creek, MI: America Healing, A Racial Equity Initiative of the W. K. Kellogg Foundation), 5.

3. Turner, *The Business Case for Racial Equity*, 6.

4. "Legal Rights & Gov't," *Slavery and the Making of America*, Thirteen Media with Impact, https://www.thirteen.org/wnet/slavery/experience/legal/docs2.html.

### Chapter 8 Defy "White Privilege"

1. Peggy McIntosh, "White Privilege: Unpacking the Invisible Knapsack," *Peace and Freedom*, July/August 1989.

2. Martin Luther King, "Letter from Birmingham City Jail" in *A Testament of Hope: The Essential Writings and Speeches of Martin Luther King, Jr.*, ed. James Melvin Washington (New York: HarperSanFrancisco, 1986), 295.

3. Wikipedia, s.v. "meritocracy," last modified March 1, 2023, https://en.wikipedia.org/wiki/Meritocracy.

4. Chris Drew, "15 Meritocracy Examples," The Helpful Professor, December 6, 2022, https://helpfulprofessor.com/meritocracy-examples/.

### Chapter 9 Abandon "Black Inferiority"

1. US Government Publishing Office, "Senate Report 114-341," https://www.govinfo.gov/content/pkg/CRPT-114srpt341/html/CRPT-114srpt341.htm.

2. Cornerstone Institute, "Morocco Restores World's Oldest University," Cornerstone, n.d., https://cornerstone.ac.za/morocco-restores-worlds-oldest-university/.

3. "The Oldest University in the World," Erudera, September 24, 2021, https://erudera.com/resources/oldest-universities/.

4. "The Oldest University," Erudera.

### Chapter 10 Appreciate Our Mosaic, Part 1

1. Henry Wadsworth Longfellow, as quoted in L. Pylodet, Augusta Harriet (Garrigue) Leypoldt, *The Literary News*, vol. 4, April 1883 (New York: F. Leypoldt, 1883), 122.

2. Lee Anne Bell, Maurianne Adams, Pat Griffin, eds., "History of Racism and Immigration Timeline: Key Events in the Struggle for Racial Equality in the

United States," in *Teaching for Diversity and Social Justice* (New York: Routledge, 2007), timeline accessed at https://eastsideforall.org/wp-content/uploads/2020/01/History-of-Racism-and-Immigration-Timeline.pdf.

3. "Hunger and Poverty in the Indigenous Community," Fact Sheet, September 2018, Bread for the World, https://www.bread.org/sites/default/files/downloads/hunger-poverty-indigenous-communities-september-2018.pdf.

## Chapter 11 Appreciate Our Mosaic, Part 2

1. Dictionary.com, s.v. "Manifest Destiny," https://www.dictionary.com/browse/manifest-destiny.

2. Bell, Adams, and Griffin, "History of Racism and Immigration Time Line."

3. Turner, *The Business Case for Racial Equity*, 4.

4. Turner, *The Business Case for Racial Equity*, 5.

5. Turner, *The Business Case for Racial Equity*, 5.

6. US Department of the Treasury Department, "Racial Differences in Economic Security: Housing," November 4, 2022, https://home.treasury.gov/news/featured-stories/racial-differences-in-economic-security-housing.

7. Turner, *The Business Case for Racial Equity*, 6.

8. History.com editors, "Manifest Destiny," *History*, updated November 15, 2019, https://www.history.com/topics/19th-century/manifest-destiny.

9. Wikipedia, s.v. "patriotism," last updated February 23, 2023, https://en.wikipedia.org/wiki/Patriotism.

## Chapter 12 Understand the Change Sequence

1. Kevin DeYoung, "10 Reasons Racism Is Offensive to God," The Gospel Coalition, June 25, 2015, https://www.thegospelcoalition.org/blogs/kevin-deyoung/10-reasons-racism-is-offensive-to-god/.

2. DeYoung, "10 Reasons Racism Is Offensive to God."

3. DeYoung, "10 Reasons Racism Is Offensive to God."

4. *Strong's Concordance* and *Thayer's Greek Lexicon*, s.v. "G3340—Repent," King James Bible Dictionary, https://kingjamesbibledictionary.com/StrongsNo/G3340/repent.

5. Heben Nigatu, "21 Racial Microaggressions You Hear on a Daily Basis," BuzzFeed, December 9, 2013, https://www.buzzfeed.com/hnigatu/racial-microagressions-you-hear-on-a-daily-basis.

6. Nigatu, "21 Racial Microaggressions."

7. Dictionary.com, s.v. "microaggression," https://www.dictionary.com/browse/microaggression.

## Chapter 13 Adopt the Change Model

1. Dr. Martin Luther King Jr. on *Meet the Press*, April 17, 1960.

2. Emmanuel Kojo Ennin Antwi, "Church Involvement in the Trans-Atlantic Slave Trade: Its Biblical Antecedent *vis-à-vis* the Society's Attitude to Wealth," *Studia Historiae Ecclesiasticae* 44, no. 2 (2018): 1–19, https://dx.doi.org/10.25159/2412 4265/3245.

3. Aryeh Bernstein, "The Torah Case for Reparations," Medium, March 29, 2018, https://aryehbernstein.medium.com/the-torah-case-for-reparations-bbe41e7763c0.

4. Dina Gerdeman, "The Clear Connection Between Slavery and American Capitalism," *Forbes*, May 3, 2017, https://www.forbes.com/sites/hbsworkingknowledge/2017/05/03/the-clear-connection-between-slavery-and-american-capitalism/?sh=1259b747bd3b.

5. Peter Scholtes, "They'll Know We Are Christians," © 1966, F.E.L. Publications, assigned to The Lorenz Corp., 1991.

6. Lynette Jachowicz, "What Is a Transactional Relationship?" Study.com, update January 14, 2022, https://study.com/learn/lesson/transactional-relationships-psychology.html.

7. Wikipedia, s.v. "Reparations (transitional justice)," last updated November 13, 2022, https://en.wikipedia.org/wiki/Reparations_(transitional_justice).

8. *Merriam-Webster*, s.v. "recompense," https://www.merriam-webster.com/dictionary/recompense.

**Skot Welch** is the principal/founder of Global Bridgebuilders (GBB), a firm focusing on organizational developments, cultural transformation, and inclusion. Global Bridgebuilders is an international team providing services to enterprises across the globe. GBB bases its work in the core belief that inclusion is a business discipline that should be leveraged across all the enterprise does. To gain this leverage, the firm applies a continuous improvement model, anchored in metrics.

Skot had been a global bridge builder long before he founded the company in 2006. Growing up in a military family gave Skot a unique perspective on diversity that he still carries and a passion for helping organizations tap into the vast experiences of their employees to create stronger businesses.

Currently, Global Bridgebuilders serves a wide range of clients in the US and other countries around the world. Skot has worked in international business and diversity/inclusion management for over twenty-five years and has developed an in-depth knowledge of diversity, inclusion, and workforce development that brings together and maximizes the perfect blend of people and process.

Prior to the launch of Global Bridgebuilders, Skot served as Vice President of Business Development and Benchmarking Services for DiversityInc magazine in New Jersey, where he worked with many of the Fortune 500's biggest global brands across a broad range of industries.

Skot is also the author of two previous books, *101 Ways to Enjoy the Mosaic: Creating a Diverse Community Right in Your*

*Own Backyard* and *Sayings: To Inspire You Along the Way (and Maybe Even Change Your Life)*; and co-author of two others, *Plantation Jesus—Race, Faith and a New Way Forward* and *The Ross School of Business–University of Michigan: Diversity Management as a Generative Strategic Process: When the Business Case Meets Positive Organizational Scholarship*.

Finally, Skot is an ordained minister with a heart for and focus on seeing the body of Christ advance and finance the kingdom of God through entrepreneurship, innovation, and cross-cultural collaboration.

My Notes

My Notes

My Notes

# My Notes

My Notes

# My Notes